Outdance the Devil is an eye-opening re traumatic life-event.....*and* for those who stories than any one man should have to (resilience offers hope to those in their darkest hour and insight to those in the margins who are there for support. A must read.

Lt John Rainier

SWAT Commander Rock Hill PD

Mark Spicer has done an incredible job writing this book. His honest, genuine and emotionally charged words have brought a heightened awareness to an issue that should concern us all. This is an absolutely must-read book. It pulls no punches, and you will cry.

Karen Hunter

Athlon Outdoors Content Writer & Firearms Instructor

I feel that a great book can stay with you forever. But, the true testament of an Amazing book is that it changes your life. I genuinely believe that Outdance the Devil will change the lives of so many. For so many people to feel they had a disorder instead of an injury will inspire so many to fight their demons in a way they didn't think was possible. Mark's bravery to reveal so much about himself is only matched by his Humility.

Lt Tony Breeden

Rock Hill PD

22 Veterans and countless civilians commit suicide EACH DAY, and I am certain that you know someone right now who is struggling with these horrible thoughts. Mark Spicer has committed to fight this battle straight on and has released his deeply autobiographical accounts in his book: "OUTDANCE THE DEVIL: A Sniper's Account of the Scariest Enemy He Ever Fought". I am proud to stand by my friend Mark and help champion suicide prevention & PTSD/PTSI, so please join the fight.

Michael Giuliano
President & Chairman of the Board - Tier One Entrepreneur

Gripping, visceral and very emotional. This brutally honest and awe-inspiring account of Mark's career and personal life is a must read for everyone. PTSI is a killer and I fully support Mark's mission to raise awareness and show that it can effect anyone. It is not a military illness.

Brian Wood MC
Veteran and Author of the best-selling book "Double Crossed"

Mark Spicer provides an insightful, gripping and very emotional tribute to the soldiers of one of the world's most elite organizations. His personal experience captures the essence of a life lived on the tip of the spear and, more importantly, the challenges faced by these warriors on their long journey home. Mark's mission to raise awareness and show that PTSD can effect anyone, first responders, medical professionals and even grieving parents is much needed and highly commendable. A must read! This book comes with my highest recommendation. Brutally honest and inspiring.

Norman Hooten
1st SFOD – Delta Veteran and Owner of Hooten Young American Whiskey

Mark Spicer's latest mission is help demystify the dark labyrinth that is Post Traumatic Stress. As a front-line veteran, he knows how combat often defines the circumstances that precipitate PTSD but he goes much deeper in this book, using personal accounts from front line veterans and emergency services to make sure, that we all understand the 'illness' rather than pontificating about the 'disorder'! I commend this book and its endeavour to help those trapped in the dark to emerge into the light.

Major Ken Hames
MBE UK Special Forces (Rtd.)

Mark is brutally honest and frank in his summation of this potentially deadly illness. His background as a professional Army combat veteran and a security contractor uniquely qualifies him to share his story and thoughts to not only those who are struggling emotionally but also to the families and loved ones who care for them 24/7. The support engine Mark is encouraging to those in need requires our undivided attention and focus on those military, first responders and civilians who have honorably served and sacrificed so much for their respective countries and communities.

Alan Brosnan New Zealand SAS (Rtd.)
President of Tactical Energetic Entry Systems (TEES)

Our society is just scratching the surface regarding the problems associated with our protectors and the PTS they experience as a result of their service. Mark's account is candid and honest. He engages personal topics once considered off limits to the soldier and only recently recognized as a legitimate injury as a result of military experience. Mark and I have been friends for over a decade having met during training in 2009. We share much in common, not least of which is the desire to bring awareness to the plight of our servicemen and women regarding their mental well-being. Outdance the Devil tears away the armor worn by so many soldiers, sailors, airmen, marines, law enforcement officers, firemen, and other protectors of our society in a way few can manage.

Travis C Denman MSG USA (Ret.)
US Army Special Operations 1992-2014

Mark shines a spotlight on a hugely important topic, and he does so in a very noble and vulnerable way. A must-read, but more importantly an urgent call to action.

Micheal Iacobucci
Col (Ret.) 75th Ranger Battalion USSOCOM.

Mark has been a prominent and respected figure in the sniping community for a number of years, and his knowledge and operational experience has made him a natural leader. I am not surprised to see Mark step up and show the courage and initiative to write about this very sensitive topic and share his experiences in hope to help others. As a soldier or a first responder there are many books that you can read to prepare yourself for your occupation, and this book should be on the top of your list.

Rob Furlong
Canadian Army Master Sniper (Ret.)

Outdance The Devil

A Sniper's Account of the Scariest Enemy He Ever Fought

By Mark Spicer

With Dr. Keerthy Sunder

Cataloged in publication information is available from Library and Archives U.S.

E-book: ISBN: 978-1-956257-47-2

Paperback: ISBN: 978-1-956257-46-5

Formatting, publishing, cover design by Pierucci Publishing

Interior design by Sophie Hanks

Edited by Dale Chaplin

Cover design by Stephanie Pierucci

You are strong alone, but together we are STRONGER.

Mark Spicer

www.outdancethedevil.com

S | T | R | O | N | G

I created an acronym that I believe will help others stay focused in dark times. I knew it had to be a common word, a word that invokes powerful images, and so I settled on the word STRONG. This wasn't enough though, so it grew to STRONGER to help maintain and convey a forward momentum. This is listed below and is a place that I believe is a natural end to my story. Know your own worth, especially in the eyes of others, and know that you are never alone. The most dangerous enemy I ever faced…was me.

Stay in the Fight
Tell Others You Need Help
Resist the Dark
Own It
Never Quit
Grow From the Pain

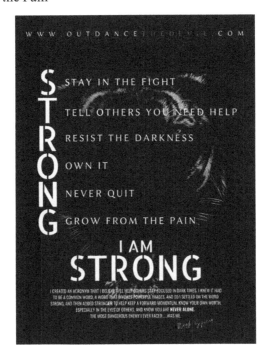

Contents

Foreword

It is with great pleasure that I write this foreword for this valuable and much-needed work.

I have had the pleasure of knowing Mark Spicer for several years, working closely with him for two of those. The veteran of Active Service in Northern Ireland and the Balkans, he is very much a "soldier's soldier", and a man that I greatly respect and have the pleasure of calling a friend and comrade.

There is a saying; "Being a civilian is easy, and being a soldier is easy. It is making the change that is hard, in either direction". Life can be hard enough, for anyone, of any age and background, but PTSD for both soldiers and civilians alike, make it exponentially so, with all too often tragic results.

Mark's worthy ambition is to help avoid such tragedy, or at the very least, extend a lifeline to those most in need, and consequently at risk, of harming themselves or others. If anyone can reach those suffering from the "silent killer" of PTSD, it is Mark Spicer, as he truly has passed through hell on earth, and emerged very still in the fight, for which we, his friends, are very grateful.

Further, if just one person finds what they need not just to survive, but to thrive, in these pages, then Mark and I both will derive more satisfaction than could ever be expressed in words. I would urge anyone who is thus afflicted to turn to these pages and to seek the help that they need so that their family and friends can also share in the gratitude that I feel and rejoice in life and survival.

His Royal Highness Prince Talal bin Muhammad of Jordan
Major-General, Jordan Arab Army (Ret.)

Our Goal to Destigmatise PTSD

I feel that it's important to note that Post-Traumatic Stress Disorder (PTSD) and Post-Traumatic Stress Injury (PTSI) are interchangeable terms for the same condition. Here, in this book, I will use the term PTSI. The term "Injury" replaces the term "Disorder" as PTSI is an injury to the mind. For example, you would not categorise a broken leg or a fractured hip as a "disorder." In the same vein, the mind of the victim of PTSI has been broken by an event, by trauma, in much the same way a physical trauma breaks a bone. Similar to breaking a bone, the wound never fully heals. The leg will always bear the scars of the break, a pain or a mark will always exist, perhaps coming and going according to how cold it is or if any stress is placed upon it. The same is true of PTSI. It never fully heals; we just learn how to treat the symptoms and manage the "break." PTSD has long been stigmatised in the media and the world of showbiz. By renaming the condition to reflect more accurately what it truly is, we address and remove the stigma attached to it and challenge the conceptions that surround it, laying the path to its treatment and its destigmatisation.

PTSI and the associated depression are devastating. You have no idea why you do what you do. You can't remember things you did; you can't see why people cannot see you are trying to ask for help but don't know how. You feel like there is no way out. You want a way out, you want to be happy, you don't want to hurt those closest to you, but you do, and each time pushes you further and further into the Darkness. You reach a calmness, a calmness of acceptance, a calmness that comes from knowing that you're the problem, and you have to go.

Twenty-two veterans a day reach that point, as well as countless civilians; PTSI doesn't care if you served. We have to do more to recognise the signs, see the character changes that warn of a path that leads to another loss of life. Learn, understand and support those who fight themselves harder than they have ever fought an enemy._

#Veterans #People #Help #22ADay #PTSD #PTSDSurvivor #PTSDAwareness #Darkness #SuicidePrevention #MilitaryFamilies #Suicide #Family #Military #Awareness #Love #Understand #SupportingEachOther

Trigger Warning: *Why I Wrote this Book*

First and foremost, I don't want this to be viewed as another book about soldiers. I want this book to show that PTSI is not a disorder; it's an illness. It does not care if you have served. This book will primarily focus on my life, and being a soldier for most of it, it's going to have a part of my career attached by necessity. That is not, however, my point, and I ask from the first page that you understand this book is for anyone who has suffered traumatic stress: the police officer who carried the dead teenager from a car; the firefighter who could not reach the child through the flames; the doctor or nurse who could not save a life or the parent who has lost a child. All of you suffer traumatic stress and so all of you may need help. I use the military because those who serve are most at risk and because that is my life - my story. Remember though, that PTSI has no favourites, it has no shame, and so I will use my experience to try and show synergy with everyone who has found themselves alone in the dark. The book may well trigger some, and so I warn you now that I cut no corners in explaining my trauma. The experts, like Dr. Sunder, whom I am blessed to know, will advise throughout the book on ways to help calm triggers, all of which have helped me in my journey. Please take a break if you find my story pushing you too far. Cry, I cry every time I read it. That's ok, it's the body's way of emptying the cup so to speak, but stress, signs of stress, anxiety, etc. must all be respected. I wish to help, not harm.

Mindfulness

For many of you reading this book, it will not be easy. For those battling Post-Traumatic Stress, this book will likely contain stories and themes that may well be triggering for you. They may well unlock some of the memories and feelings that have allowed Post-Traumatic Stress to take hold of your psyche and do its work.

Others of you may be living with and loving those that are suffering from Post-Traumatic Stress, hoping to understand more about their struggle and help them, and yourself, along the journey. Perhaps gaining insight from someone who has fought, and is still fighting the same battle, may cause you some upset and empathy for those you love.

Others of you may have a professional or personal curiosity, wanting to understand more about a condition that has long been stigmatised by Western societies. The media, cinema and television have done a lot to harm the perception of Post-Traumatic Stress and those that suffer from it, portraying them often as crazed individuals that actively pursue self-damaging behaviours, or behaviours that harm others.

For all of you, this book is going to ask a lot of you. It is going to ask for understanding. It is going to ask you to confront pain, both in yourself and in others, and it is going to ask you to cast aside some of what you think you know about Post-Traumatic Stress and its impact on those both suffering and caring for those that suffer. It is not going to be an easy read.

As such, I feel that it is important that I introduce myself. My name is Dr. Keerthy Sunder, an Integrative Psychiatrist. My team and I have over 20 years of experience in working with and helping to treat those suffering from Post-Traumatic Stress with mindfulness, neurotechnology and gut-brain modulation. I know that for many of the people we have worked with, the steps they have taken and the work we have done with and for them has been life changing. In particular, our work focuses on the impact of mindfulness on those suffering from Post-Traumatic Stress, and how it can be used to both alleviate and treat some of the internal and external symptoms and effects of Post-Traumatic Stress.

At the end of this book, you will find an article written by me. This article pulls together clinical studies that prove the positive impact that mindfulness has on those that suffer from Post-Traumatic Stress. I urge you to read it. Each of the studies has been fully referenced, so I encourage you to take a look at those also.

I want to introduce you to this concept at the start of this book, as I believe that it will help in the reading of this book. Practising some of the mindfulness techniques that my team and I recommend whenever you feel like you need to stop or take a break may just give you the strength to continue, and the continuation of these practices after may just change your life.

'The practice of mindfulness is rooted in reflective traditions that seek increased awareness through meditation. The main aim of mindfulness is to cultivate an attitude of compassion and curiosity to the present moment.' So, what did you read into that? If you're anything like many of those that I have spoken to and came before you, you saw the word meditation and immediately switched off. After all, your mind is so busy, how on earth could meditation work? That's the problem, isn't it? You can't get your mind to switch off!

What if I told you that it is not about getting your mind to switch off. What if, instead of it being about mental silence, it's about confronting what is happening in your mind– on your terms. It is about being aware of yourself; where you are, what you are thinking, and reflecting and making sense of all of that. It is not about silencing the mind, it is about listening to it, it is about being an observer and truly understanding what is going on.

For a sufferer of Post-Traumatic Stress, this is crucial. This will be discussed in detail later in the book, but when you suffer from Post-Traumatic Stress, in your mind, the problem is not you, it's everyone else around you. Nobody seems to understand you, or your way of looking at things, so they are inherently wrong. Mindfulness helps tackle this, allowing you to address when actually, you, as the sufferer, may be in the wrong. Or, enabling you to reflect on challenging situations, learning from your mistakes or preventing them from happening in the first place.

It is also worth noting that mindfulness is not just about meditation, 'This concept appears in the form of meditation and consists of two categories: physical body movement and mindfulness meditation.' This physical body movement suits many of those who are most prone to Post-Traumatic Stress; military and emergency personnel. Many of these people have lived an active lifestyle, so techniques like Yoga, Tai Chi or Qigong may well come more naturally to them. They may even, and often do, open the door to meditation. The important thing is that these practices will offer you a physical outlet for your feelings, and will help to guide and centre you, making you aware of your energy and that of others.

Mindfulness Reduces Post-Traumatic Stress Symptom Severity

Mindfulness allows us to confront our memories. In particular, it allows us to confront the attitudes and feelings that these memories have anchored onto. Studies prove it, with veterans suffering from PTS self-reporting significant reductions in symptoms and substantial improvements in their quality of life after just 8 weeks of twice-weekly treatment sessions. In addition, this has been proven clinically, with a mindfulness-based cognitive therapy (MBCT) program finding meaningful decreases in symptom severity.

So what does this mean? In short, these studies demonstrated that mindfulness helps those suffering from PTS. In particular, it helps with two key symptoms: avoidance/numbing symptoms, and the tendency to self-blame. It is these symptoms in particular that can lead to the damaging of relationships and potential suicidal/self-harming behaviours.

Mindfulness Helps Combat Addiction and Substance Abuse

It is no secret that many of those suffering from PTS turn to drugs, alcohol and other substances to help them cope. PTS can shut down the parts of the brain we use to feel, or it can wake them up in a way that feels to the victim like a mental overload. As a result, sufferers may turn to substances to either make them feel more, or to make them feel less.

Mindfulness also has this effect. When the mind is in that frantic stage, mindfulness can help to slow that down and process this in the correct way for the individual. Likewise, when the sufferer is struggling to feel anything at all, it can help them in their awareness of that, unlocking those parts of the brain that we use to experience emotions.

Furthermore, "In a recent study of veterans with comorbid PTSD and alcohol use disorder, an 8-week mindfulness-based stress reduction program resulted in significant symptom reduction, with benefit retention in areas including depression, behavioural activation, acceptance, and mindfulness at 6 month-follow-up." Mindfulness helps sufferers to do what they otherwise may rely on alcohol to do for them, allowing them to overcome addiction, or avoid it in the first place.

Mindfulness has Been Used for Centuries, and Many Clinics are Coming Back to it

Mindfulness has been used in many cultures throughout the world for centuries. Long before the existence of modern medicine and brain scans, our ancestors had to find ways to manage and cope with the same conditions we have today, albeit under different names. They turned to mindfulness.

In the modern world, we have combined mindfulness with medicine to create programs specifically for those that need them, according to their situation. Remember, Post-Traumatic Stress is an injury to the brain, and we can use brain scans and EEG to study the changes in the brain that has undergone trauma. We have also witnessed the effects of mindfulness using these same scans; "As science catches up with tradition, sensitive imaging techniques enable the visualisation of physiological changes as they occur in the brains and bodies of mindfulness practitioners, providing scientific proof where previously only empirical evidence existed." There is abundant evidence that demonstrates the healing properties of mindfulness, with the concept gaining traction in the wider medical community.

So, why have I told you all of this? It's because I believe, based on my own experience and those of the people I have helped, that this will help you. It will not only help you progress through this book, but it will also help you after, as you continue your battle with Post-Traumatic Stress and its many symptoms.

For those of you loving and living with sufferers of Post-Traumatic Stress, you may be able to help those you love to begin this journey. You may even find this works for you, both with your own stresses and challenges and those brought about by caring for someone with Post-Traumatic Stress.

And for those of you with an academic or personal curiosity, understanding and being aware of these techniques and practices will help promote them, bringing the proven benefits to many others, and maybe even yourself.

Remember, the article is in the appendix of this book. I encourage you to read it.

Transitioning from Soldier to Civilian

There's a way to get soldiers out from behind the rock under which they've been dodging bullets - but it isn't easy. Transitioning from Soldier to Civilian is a complex phenomenon that we've failed at facilitating.

You see, when you become a civilian, you're still a Soldier. You don't stop looking at every garbage can or bin you pass like it's going to explode. The nightmares don't stop. You still feel the breath of death or fear down your neck. You're hyper-alert, impulsive, sleepless… and angry.

All of these are the results of the army having necessarily deconstructed and reconstructed you to transform you into a Soldier, fit for duty. However, when you leave the Service, you're given 2-4 weeks of training to be a plumber or labourer; but what you really need is to reconstruct your psyche.

When you leave the Service, you immediately realise that something ain't right; and that something, is you. You spend a lot of time in both metaphorical and physical Darkness.

Maybe you reach out and call a mate who's still a soldier. These guys were your support system. In so many ways, they were and are your lifeline. But they're still soldiers. In order to stay alive, they don't stop to feel.

They respond the only way they know how, "Man up, brother. You've got this, you just gotta soldier on." You feel better for five minutes and then don't call again because, even though they're your brothers, you feel like you're a burden to them, a failure. The Darkness reappears quickly, and now you're more alone than ever. Even your humour doesn't fit in with civilian life. You've seen so much, and people don't understand why you laugh at morbid shit. It disturbs people, but that's how you deal with stress. You're not fitting in. Even the family you dreamt of every second of your Service doesn't know how to relate to you anymore. That rejection is gutting; another nail in your coffin.

Remember, you've been completely deconstructed from the person that was somebody's husband, son, or brother. You've been re-moulded into a Soldier. The very therapy you need would have made you weak and unfit for service. You've been brainwashed into thinking that it's wrong to seek help.

For soldiers, not being okay means vulnerability, and even death. As a civilian, you must learn to be okay with not being okay; to seek help, and to continue serving humanity by first saving yourself.

Soldiers are trained to find solutions, because failure is death. But what keeps you alive in the army will kill you as a civilian, and vice versa.

But a problem we haven't yet solved is the problem of PTSI and loneliness among our Veterans.

Soldiers are not frightened by the fight in front of them, they are frightened of the fight that's behind them. Keeping it together, being brave on deployment, is easy, because you want to get home to those you love. It's when you get home, and you can't fit in, that you collapse. Those you love have not seen what you have seen, not felt what you have felt, how could they, and it's impossible to put into words.

The Darkness is Not Your Friend

"What the hell do I want to talk about my childhood for? I said, almost snarling. "I want to know how to win my wife back!"

My very first thoughts at having been asked about what my first childhood memories were during my first ever therapy session, turned out to be the key that opened the door, the flip of a switch that turned on the light, showing me a direction, a path that I had to take. A path that, up to this point, I had resisted, ignored, pretended didn't exist. It was, however, a path I knew inside was not only there, but one I was meant to follow. It was a primal path that opened my eyes to struggle, to pain, many, many tears and to my feelings about God. The path I was about to take showed me who I really was. It allowed me to close a door behind me. The path I was about to walk down would be a path that led me home.

My wife had walked out on me. On her way out the door, she'd listed all my failings, everything I had ever done...all wrong...that had led to her leaving. Over the next six months, I met a therapist two to three times a week to delve into whether or not it truly was all my fault and to put right whatever I was doing wrong. My mission: to win my wife back.

Yet as those therapy sessions went on, I was to discover that, in fact, it was my wife who had issues. It was my wife who had been cheating on me with that fellow teacher. Cheating on me for two of the three years we had been married. I discovered, found out, realised, that her narcissistic actions were projected upon me as camouflage to cover their adultery. She was gaslighting me. That's the truth I discovered. The depth of this betrayal will get its coverage later in this book, right now all I will say is that it added to the self-belief scars I already carried. Right now, all I will say is that her actions allowed the dark waves of PTSI to once again invade my thoughts. Right now, all I will say is that her betrayal distorted my view of people and ended up hurting the people I loved.

My life had all but collapsed around me for the second time in a fairly short period of my life. The first was the sudden and abrupt end of my previous marriage. The second - my wife leaving - dragged me back to a very cold place, a place so cold and silent. I found myself in a familiar, unwelcome place, one that I had, unfortunately, spent considerable time in before. It was... is... a place where nothing penetrated, not reason, not hope, not love, not responsibility... Nothing.

I existed in a place of Darkness that, while I could see out to the world, its sunlight, people, life going on around me, nothing, or no one, can see into. All they can see of you is an image. An image that they either choose themselves or an image your mind's defensive nature portrays to better keep everyone away from you. When you are in that dark place, you are really controlled by the Darkness. The Darkness designed the place, and so within, it reigns. The Darkness becomes your lens, leading you to believe it's your friend.

It's a sort of addiction that keeps you encased in a heavy blanket, a blanket of thought. Too much thought. Too much dark thinking that leads to more dark thinking, thick with despair and almost sticky in its encapsulation of you. It tricks you, allowing you to think you are moving freely, but in reality, it is holding your soul ransom, a hostage to the images and thoughts it projects onto the theatre of your minds-eye.

Within the casket-box of Darkness that is the despair of PTSI, your life, love and reasons for being are slashed like something from a horror film. You may feel like the Darkness is your best friend, a sort of salvation. It is not. It is only a protective addiction your mind creates, a camouflage world where light is prevented from entering. A Darkness that camouflages itself as a path back to light. It tells you to trust it, that if you do it will ease your pain, remove your burdens and free you again. This is the dark place that leads to PTSI related suicides, a place that only leads to the ruin of so many lives by pulling a blinding shade over your eyes and your soul while you are a prisoner of your pride.

They spend six months training you to be a soldier. In contrast, they only give two weeks at the end of your career on instructing you how best to fit back into society, a society that doesn't understand you, doesn't want you, doesn't care what you have just sacrificed to ensure their lives have the free will they believe they are entitled to.

Then you get back home. Back to the wife. Back to the kids. Back to the routine. Only, it's different from what you're used to, and it's different from what your wife is used to. You aren't welcomed home like the hero you are. Like Agamemnon after Troy, sometimes you come back to a home in pieces. You try your best. You get up in the morning and brush your teeth.

You read the paper, try to not get under your wife's feet, try not to drink too much. But, as the days accumulate, the Darkness that whispers in your ear may seem like more and more of an option, perhaps the only way. Suicidal thoughts, like a dripping tap…drip… drip, don't ever fully go away.

"Go now!" Those thoughts say, "Do it – while you still have something left - pride, dignity - goddammit! Go out on your terms!"

Truth is, the act of taking your life under this type of thinking is not something done on your own terms. No, killing yourself under these circumstances is not done on your terms, but on the terms of the Darkness. And those terms exact a toll on those you leave behind. You leave behind a debt.

A debt you simply cannot repay.

In some sense, all you do when you take your life amid the throes of PTSI is pass the torch of Darkness along to the next soul. That soul is the soul of someone you love. Suicide is not cowardly, but it is selfish. Selfish beyond reason And it allows the Darkness to perpetuate.

Now, I don't believe in the devil or hell, at least not as described by the Bible or any other doctrine. I don't believe in fallen Archangels, the river Styx or Dante's Inferno. If Satan is a thing, a being, I believe it is in us. Or rather, it can be in us. I believe that the devil and hell exist in our own minds, in how we choose to see things. We can rot in eternity in our own thoughts because the Darkness is a patient entity. It bides its time, patiently waiting for that moment when life comes down hard on its host and, like the snake in the Garden of Eden, strikes.

The Darkness strikes as a fear. Franklin Delano Roosevelt told us that, "the only thing we need to fear is fear itself." While I'm not big on quoting government officials outside of Churchill, I do think old FDR got that one right. He is right because fear is a sickness. Fear is an addiction. Fear gets you killed, and fear gets you to kill yourself.

How? Because it suffocates you as a smoke-filled tunnel does. It blinds you to thought and reason, while you stumble around looking for clean air and a way to escape. The reason you instinctively place your hand on the light switch at home is that you are familiar with your surroundings, and so you know where to reach for the light. PTSI grips you in an unfamiliar Darkness and many fail to find the switch, stumbling further into the Darkness until they are lost.

Many people succumb to this devil within, unable to find a light to lead them out. Soldiers… ex-soldiers in particular.

For some reason, every time I have been in the Darkness, I have managed to find a light, the light, and pull my way out.

But I am no hero. I'm nothing special, so why me? Why have I been able to do this while others I have served with took their lives? In truth, I don't know. What I do know is that I feel a deep drive that I have something to do. Maybe this book is it, and after this, I can rest.

I feel I have to go on, I have to tell my story, I have to tell it so that someone else may read it and learn that there is always light. There is always another way other than suicide. I haven't killed myself because deep inside I know that there is more to do.

Maybe I am just the egomaniac people have accused me of being in the past. Maybe on some subconscious level, it's all just about stroking my ego. I don't think so, but I'll let you be the judge. On some level, I will have to let you decide my fate, for, at this time, I have no answers – only more questions.

This book will not be about some soldier, not about some sniper rattling off how brave he is. Nah, this book is just about a boy who grew up in a council house in Portsmouth, Hampshire. The Brit who left school at 16 and had to learn how to survive in the real world. Just a poor lad with big dreams, who somehow survived multiple deployments, and who ended up mingling with Kings, Princes and movie stars.

This is a simple book about a man who lost himself too many times to count, but who has never stopped listening to the guiding voice within, led by the deep desire to do the right thing. A book about a man who failed that desire on more occasions than he cares to remember, but who has got back up more times than he has been knocked down. A man who found that everything he wanted in life was always just behind fear, and that courage is not the absence of fear; it is not letting fear stop you.

It is a man's drive to find that one thing we all subconsciously look for; the meaning of our lives. While I have yet to find it, I do feel I now have a better understanding of it because of my failings, my life's tragedies and finding my own path to my God.

Now, at this stage, if you have been reading this considering if it's worth some of your hard-earned money, you may well now be considering putting it back on the shelf as the last thing you want is another God Squad book. I can promise you; it's not that. In fact, many men and women of God will not like or agree with much I am about to write, but it is not their journey I am going to describe; it's mine. It's *my* path, *my* take on God and how it has affected me and those around me. How it fits into my perception of life and its meaning for me. Why I believe in God and yet I have serious reservations about organised religion.

It is about my failings. It is about the people I have hurt, the people I have let down, the people I have taken advantage of for my own personal gain, and also the people who have hurt me, let me down and taken advantage of me. How each one, whilst separate, could be viewed as a necessary event to push me back to, or even progress through the path that I am destined to take. It is about how, though my life events and tragedies have escaped explanation to me - even though I have searched and reasoned - I now see them as a gift.

I also know that the words in this book will be interpreted differently by every single person who reads them. Each person will associate them with their own lives and beliefs, which is normal, and I believe necessary, for it to reach and maybe help others. I will also describe events as seen through my eyes, and so it may vary considerably from how those involved saw it. And that's ok as well; the only way to learn - to grow - is to see yourself through the eyes of others as well as your own. So, let's face it, we all tend to see the person we would choose to be, and that is often not who the world sees or who we really are at that time, and so I accept this is a one-sided view and so, very possibly, it is wrong. It is just the thoughts and reasoning of one man, one soul, not perfect, not special, just looking for a reason to go on like everyone else.

So far in my life, I have witnessed suicide, the unexpected loss of my father, I have been blown up, I have betrayed, and I have been betrayed. I have let friends down and I have been let down by friends, I have seen best friends murdered, others lie for their own benefit and turn on each other for money. I watch day-to-day as, one-by-one, great soldiers and men lose their battles to the likes of cancer and PTSI after surviving so much risk and hardship.

This often leads me to wonder why I am still here. As I've said, the truth is, I don't know and while, like everyone, I struggle at times, my deep belief in a higher being - God, Life, The Universe - whatever you choose to call it, has always held me up. Sometimes, it was a call from a friend out of the blue, an email, a chance meeting. Sometimes it's a song on the radio whose lyrics answer the very question I just asked in myself in my mind, or a scent that breaks my mood and takes me to another place, another person. Sometimes I just cannot explain it past a feeling; like I am being physically held up.

Whatever it is, it has never failed me yet and I guess if the day comes where I truly stop believing, I will fall and stop trying to get up. I just can't see that day ever happening and so I must go on and view each hardship as a lesson, a nudge or a wake-up call. I take each day as it comes, and if it gets Dark and I stumble,

I work once again to find the light. So far, I have succeeded, and I am hoping that maybe my struggles, my battles in the Dark, can help others to stand back up when it feels impossible.

As I said before, my life is not over yet and I have no doubts that as I write this, events and chapters will add themselves to this story. I will write and maybe rewrite as the writing brings to light deeper memories than perhaps are available to me today. It is by no means intended as a guide or example of anything, it is merely a summary of the successes and failures of one man as he stumbled through life and that may, in some small way, be of use to others. I do not have the answers to what is right or wrong. I cannot tell you what is good or what is evil, as those are perceived differently in every situation and person. I can only illustrate my perceptions.

My life, like anyone else's, is a combination of all things. In life, there can be no up, without down. Without failure, there can be no success, and certainly, as is most poignant in my life, if you don't get knocked down, you can never learn how to get back up.

This book is about my journey - my desire, and often failure, to live life by just doing the right thing. While we may not always like or choose it, we all know inside what the right thing is. Sometimes, it may set you aside from the popular group. Sometimes, it may set you at odds with current trends or social leanings, but inside we still know it's the right thing, and as a million memes tell us daily, it's better to walk alone, in the right direction, than with a crowd, heading in the wrong direction.

Doing the right thing has the ability to be a true challenge to our moral courage and can often cause stress and division. I believe that our lives are about us, not the world, us, and how we develop when faced with the options placed in our path, options we often create or put ourselves in through greed or lack of thought.

To me, it's how we cope, stand back up and move forward again that is the guide to our progress, and I hope that one man's success and failure can help others to decide upon their own path.

A path that suits the lessons they seek, and in a manner that they choose for themselves to experience. My life so far is by no means a shining path to enlightenment. Nor is it meant to be seen as some guide. I commit my experiences to paper at the suggestion of many friends who have shared or seen my troubled path, have told me how it could help others and, while I may not be convinced, they have encouraged me to write my story and let others decide if they can avoid some of my pitfalls, armed with the knowledge of what they did to me, both inside and out.

I am no saint. I have done things I am ashamed of. I have not been a good man. I have more skeletons in my closet than a Victorian grave-robber, and I know I'm not perfect. I know my past is a trail of mistakes, but it is also the story of a man facing up to his failures, a man trying to make amends and become a better version of himself every day. It is the story of a man who, whenever he seems to finally be on the path to happiness, has it ripped away like an empty crisp packet in a storm and is forced to re-evaluate his beliefs, his faith and who he really is.

Each time, I have emerged stronger, better able to forgive and see past my own anger and pain, and to spend less and less time fighting the Darkness. I am able to better see the pain in others who have caused my pain and empathise with their struggle. If my life is to have any meaning, maybe it's that the path I have followed has led me from lesson to lesson, empowering me to be better able to help others, and maybe even change outlooks on an illness that was created by traumatic life events and perpetuated by society's continued lack of understanding, a society that claims to be "woke" and supportive. This is, sadly, a lie the men and women suffering from PTSI see through, and a lie that helps the Darkness embrace and carry away 22 veterans a day.

PTSI and the associated depression are both devastating and debilitating. You have no idea why you do what you do. You cannot remember things you did, you cannot see why people, especially those closest to you, cannot see that you are trying to ask for help but don't know how. You feel like there is no way out.

You want a way out.

You want to be happy.

You do not want to hurt those closest to you.

But you do, and each time it happens it pushes you further and further into the Darkness.

You eventually reach a calmness, a calmness of acceptance. A calmness that comes from knowing that you are the problem, and you have to go.

22 veterans a day, and countless other civilians, reach that point every single day.

PTSI does not care whether or not you have served, and so my aim is to try and expose the tragedy that is happening around us, and that the majority of society does not see or understand. How could they, when its inner Darkness has been dismissed too often and they haven't felt the level of despair that hides in that Darkness?

An illegal immigrant gets arrested and the world's media lights up like the 4th of July, but a veteran, a first responder, or a mother who lost a child taking their own lives never gets a word. We have to do more to recognise the signs, to see the slight character changes that warn of a path that leads to another lost life. We owe it to the veterans, and we owe it to each other to try harder to understand and support those who fight themselves harder than they ever fought an enemy.

Finally, this book is the story of our shared drive to find meaning to life. A meaning in our often-unfulfilling lives, and while I do not hold all the answers, it is precisely because of all my failings and tragedies that I've asked lots of questions of myself.

I've been a soldier.

I've been a husband.

I've been a sniper.

I've lived.

I've looked death in the face.

I've witnessed the resurrection of lives considered too broken to go on.

I've seen the face of Post-Traumatic Stress Disorder.

I've seen it in my friends, and I've seen it in the mirror.

I've seen the statistics—that every day 22 veterans commit suicide.

And I hope I can help lower that number.

Diane

Calling her name and the silence that followed has haunted me to this day. It is the only aspect I still have trouble talking about. I'm a soldier, have been all my life, so I am very familiar with the sound of a gunshot, and yet I clearly remember an immediate mental attempt to convince myself I had heard otherwise.

For me, stories of the world slowing, or the brain processing at an alarming rate were true. I can remember, in slow motion, looking down the corridor leading to our bedroom and immediately looking at the picture frames that line the wall, family pictures, hoping to see a broken frame on the floor telling me I'd heard wrong.

There wasn't one.

The time between hearing the shot and me exploding out of my chair and running towards the bedroom can only have been a matter of one to two seconds, and yet I remember calling her name, pausing through the silence and looking for broken glass or the wood of a frame on the floor as I erupted out of my chair. I vaguely remember seeing our two German Shepherds, already at full speed, heading towards the bedroom as I followed, calling her name over and over.

———————————◆

It was a chilly morning for Phoenix. I stood outside our home, watching the black BMW that Di loved so much pulling further away. It was not unusual for me to stand in the street waving at family or friends as they drove away, so waving at Diane and her parents as they drove off to the airport was normal enough. A habit I no doubt developed from my mum, who, to this day, still stands in her doorway and waves until she can no longer see you. I have been that way my whole life. I hate saying goodbye. I remember the knot I felt in my chest as I stood on the platform of the train station, watching the train that took my son back to college, and away from me until I could no longer see it. The memory of Di's precious car turning right and out of sight is as clear today as it was on the 5ᵗʰ of August, 2009.

The day had started normally enough. We woke up early to say goodbye to Diane's parents who had come out to visit from South Carolina for a week, and she had left early to drive them to the airport and then onto work.

I didn't go straight into work that day as I normally would. The pool in our new home was greener than Robin Hood's leggings, and as you can imagine, we were desperate to use our new pool and jacuzzi, so we had a pool guy coming over to give them a look over and an assessment. I was the first person in my family to own a pool. Not a huge issue in Arizona, but for a kid from Portsmouth, it was a big deal! As it happens, the pool guy was an idiot and a total waste of my time and money. On reflection, I suppose he was probably the first red flag to a day that would change everything about me.

I called Di about two hours later to make sure they'd made their plane and she was safe at work. My heart sank the second she spoke. I had become used to the slurring voice and what it told me, and so to hear her slur, albeit very slightly, was a turn I really could have done without, especially knowing she had just reached work. I was aware of the friction between Di and the owner's daughter, so this could only make things worse. I was not, however, aware of just how bad it was.

———————————◆

I first became aware of the pattern months before, when we were sitting down to watch an episode of Cold Case files or some other police-related series on TV. I'd met Diane while she was a Police Officer on a United Nations Tour in Kosovo, and like me, she loved her job. Needless to say, our evening TV usually consisted of any show related to real-world policing. Diane would never watch a police drama, for exactly the same reasons that I wouldn't watch a TV show about soldiers. The inaccuracies would drive her mad, but Cold Case Files, Bad Boys... these were the staples of our evenings.

The only other common theme was those reality programs about the weird or unlikely…the 600lb man who needed the Fire Brigade to take him to hospital, or the woman with boobs so big she couldn't walk!

"You gotta look, it's like a car wreck!" I can hear her saying at my argument to change channels, but the giggle and her southern accent always won the day and sure enough, she was right, it was bloody fascinating!

I had first started to detect a slight slur to Diane's voice months before that night, and considering we only drank Michelob Ultra at the time, which is the equivalent of drinking a non-alcoholic beer, the suspiciousness that a life fighting terrorism will give you kicked in, and without a word, I began to watch and take note. As the night continued and we enjoyed our program, I noticed a deepening of the slur, yet we had only knocked back three beers each and, being my wife, a former cop and a southern belle, I knew Di could drink! Something wasn't adding up.

Over the next few days, I noticed that whenever she went to the bathroom, instead of walking three yards to our right and the nearest bathroom, she walked all the way back to the master bedroom. A phrase the British Army hammers into soldiers on counter-terrorism deployments is, "Absence of the normal; Presence of the abnormal." This was not normal, and my suspicions grew. Did my wife have alcohol issues?

The next time I needed a piss, I copied Di, and without raising attention, walked back into our room. I knew I had limited time and so, without entering the en-suite, I went straight to our closet. I reasoned that if something was hidden, it would be somewhere she believed I wouldn't look. Somewhere like her collection of Coach purses on the shelves. She was, of course, spot-on, a place of zero interest to the average man. But years of watching terrorists meant that I didn't think like the average man. A quick search soon yielded my worst fears, several empty mini-bar-sized bottles of Smirnoff. My heart sank.

As a soldier, you are trained that time is of the essence and to tackle issues head-on. So I walked back to the living room where Di was sitting with the pups on our sofa. I knew that she would look up as I cleared the corner and came into view. Basic human instinct is to look when the eye catches peripheral movement, and so she would not be able to stop herself from looking. With this knowledge, I came into view with the bottles in hand. I raised the bottles and asked her if she had something she wanted to tell me?

I still remember the look of utter shame on her face for the split second before she lit me up. The denial and anger I was expecting, but the look of pure disappointment in her eyes I was not. It put an immediate dent in my assumption. She shouted at me, called me names, furiously denied that she had a drinking problem, which was made worse by the fact that I offered to drink and go to counselling with her if she did have a problem, just as long as she promised to withhold no more secrets. To me, the evidence was there, plain to see. It was there in the slurring, the empty vodka bottles, the denial, but it somehow did not add up, I was missing something, and I could already feel it eating away at me. I was missing, something and I knew it.

A strength, maybe a curse, of my lifestyle and character is that I have to find answers, I cannot relax until I have as many parts of a puzzle as I can find to better analyse the facts and draw a logical conclusion, backed with every other feasible possibility. I have to have a plan. Plan A can be modified quickly into Plan B, but if you have no plan A to begin with, you lose time - vital time - and you risk losing the war. I had unanswered questions, but that night was not the time to search or ask. An impasse had already been reached.

Many people have mistaken my patience for a lack of interest or confirmation of their own ability to deceive. This is always a mistake. I can be completely devoid of patience at times, as many can attest. Drive with me for five miles with idiots sitting in the outside lane who won't let you pass and you will see my lack of patience, but what I do possess is a very deep level of self-control. A level that can last years until the right moment presents itself. And so, the game began that night; a normal day-to-day existence on the outside, but an internal monitoring for any and every indication that all was not as it seemed. This is a good skill to have as a soldier, but it is a terrible burden in a relationship where self-doubt has already hidden fear inside you. A fear that causes hyper-vigilance. A fear that often sees what is not there. A fear that leads to you hurting those you love.

There were to be several occasions when her ability to hide was outmatched by my ability to find. The British Army conducts a very detailed covert search course for units that will serve in covert surveillance roles in the world of counter-terrorism. These courses train soldiers to gain entry into a building, commercial or residential, occupied or unoccupied, and search the premises using only night-vision and associated skills to search for weapons, munitions, physical evidence or booby traps. My intrinsic knowledge of the instinctive places people hide "valuables" meant Di had little chance of concealing empty bottles, and so the inevitable questions, accusations and rows would ensue.

It was confusing for me. I'd had alcoholics in my own family and, upon reading up on the symptoms and things to look out for, it just was not adding up. Diane would be totally sober, focused and her normal self 99% of the time, so I was starting to search for other reasons. I first noticed a connection to work when I found Di sitting in our car, close to tears, one mid-afternoon during a working day and while she professed her well-being, it was clear something at work was not right.

Diane was a very experienced Police Officer when we met, having served almost 12 years with Rock Hill PD, Greenville PD, and then Greenville County Sheriff's Office before taking up a role as a United Nations Police Officer in war-torn Kosovo.

One of the many things I found attractive about her was the sheer determination, bordering on arrogance, that she had in all that she did. To those who never truly knew her and her inner self-doubt, she could be perceived as arrogant and opinionated, but this was her self-defence mechanism. Bullied from an early age, the youngest of four children with a considerable age gap between her and her middle sister, Diane spent most of her childhood with either her mum or her horses.

Horses were her passion, and they were also her safe space. As her experience grew, Diane built up a reputation for being able to ride and handle even the biggest and most aggressive of horses and was soon winning eventing competitions. Her skill was plain to see. It was a skill that was to stay with her until her all too short life was taken, eventually earning her try-outs for the US Olympic team. I never knew her as a child, but we spent many nights just talking about it. To a boy from a council house in Portsmouth, her life was a fascinating mixture of the Wild West and an American TV show in my eyes.

I was also lucky enough to spend time with her parents Roosevelt and Betty, two of the most loving and generous people I have ever met. They seemed to have a never-ending line of stories about her childhood, and their own childhoods, that held me fascinated for hours. Mind you, for the first years it was always a one-way conversation between me and Roosevelt, as I would explain something or tell him one of my own stories, where he would sit transfixed to my tale right up to the punchline when he would look at Di and say, "what did he say?"

I was to learn that Churchill was 100% right when he said that the UK and America were one nation divided by a common language, because we both certainly speak a different language at times!

Diane never really developed confidence until she became a Police Officer. She grew at college and steadily transformed from being the "ugly duckling" to a stunner who turned heads wherever she went, but outside of horses, she still struggled to believe in herself. Her strength came from two main sources, her mum, Betty, who would be her strength all her life, and her best friend and fellow horse nut Amy, both of whom helped fill in the blanks for me in the early part of mine and Diane's relationship.

———————◆

On hearing a slight slur, I took a deep breath and said, "Diane, please tell me you haven't had a drink?"

I knew she was going to be upset at her parents leaving, Di was always extremely close to her mum. They shared a sense of humour, as well as a love of Stephen King books and horror movies in general. Her mum leaving would have an effect, and so Di feeling down I had planned for.

I was planning on taking her out for dinner to the local bar for some hot wings - her go-to bar food - to help cheer her up. Diane had sworn she had not had a drink, and was predictably angry at the suggestion she had, making the conversation tense and leading to her telling me she was at work and had to go. I ended the call by telling her that if she had, to make an excuse and come home before it was noticed and she got fired. After all, it was that job and certain people in it that had caused this turn of events, but I will explain as we progress.

She hung up and I went about my morning, waiting for the pool man to arrive. Less than an hour later, she texted me to say she was not feeling well and was taking the day off sick. I remember feeling both relief and disappointment– relieved she was not about to get bullied further if it was noticed but disappointed that she had slipped back into her "pain-numbing" routine.

I remember seeing her drive past me– our BMW was hard to miss, especially with a gorgeous blond driving it– on the AZ State 303 as I drove to work once the pool idiot was done. I distinctly remember the rush of excitement I always got when I saw her. She was almost home and somewhere I knew she would be safe. Mr. Oi and little Miss Ey, our German Shepherds, would be so happy to see their mum and I knew they were a nailed-on way to cheer her up.

——————————◆

Now, I guess for the story's sake and to better explain the role both dogs and those to follow played in all of this, I should explain their names! Diane and I bought Oi from a high-end breeder in the south of England for £2,500, and he swiftly became the baby we never had together.

We were first in line, and so on our arrival at the breeder, we were shown a kennel full of the cutest little furballs you've ever seen. It was clear that we were gonna be in for a difficult choice! Long-haired German Shepherd pups are literal balls of fluff, and so for Diane, it was cuteness overload! While taking a good look at the pups, I felt a tugging on my jeans and looked down to find another puppy, outside the kennel, busying himself on saving me from my jeans. The owner, an attractive woman around Di's age (whom I was saddened to learn a few years ago had died of cancer way too early in her life), immediately explained that he had escaped somehow from a holding crate as he was the runt of the litter and she'd assumed that we wouldn't want him.

On hearing this, Diane and I looked at each other, looked back down at the pup, who had been hidden away for his lack of form, had somehow escaped, and was now showing enough charisma to fill a football stadium, looked back at each other and in harmony said, "we'll take him."

A major part of the contract with this breeder was that you had to return with the pup at the six-month stage, and if she believed you weren't taking proper care of the dog, she legally had the right to take the dog back without a refund. This was a clause I was happy to sign, as it demonstrated the love she had for her dogs and their welfare. Six months later, at the "puppy party," Oi displayed a clear recollection of how his siblings muscled him out, as he was now the biggest of all of them and spent the afternoon showing them all who was boss now!

So, when it came to naming him, it was clear, being English, that whatever we called him it would almost always be prefaced by the attention-getting word of "OI," as in "Oi Rex," or "Oi, Bear," so we made the ground-breaking decision to cut out the middleman, so to speak, and just call him Oi. Or Mr. Oi, on formal occasions.

At first, this was a decision many disagreed with for the first few months but grew to see the genius in it with time. Once we had moved to the United States with Oi and were settled into a routine, we decided that Oi needed a friend, as he spent a lot of time alone while we worked. Diane began to search the local area for a breeder.

It all eventually led us to a woman's home, about 50 miles from our house, who had a litter of pure black German Shepherds. I can honestly say I never wanted a black shepherd and vocalised that en-route. I was not even sold when I met the pups, who all seemed scrawny and undersized, but Diane was insistent, and even deadset on a particular pup. It was clear that I was not going to win this battle, and the pup came home with us.

During the trip home, Diane did the math while reading the paperwork and we realised that she was way too young to be away from her mother and, after a call to our vet, the decision was made to hand feed her as the breeder clearly could not be trusted. I ended up as the new puppy's mum.

I had more flexibility in my job than Diane, which saw me bottle feed and cradle the new pup for the first few weeks of her life, creating a bond that remained until recently when we lost her at the age of 13.

Now, considering how we named Oi, she had to have a similar name and so, in the US, to get someone's attention you would call "Hey, you!" or just "Hey!" so we dropped the H and she became Ey, or Miss Ey! I am a great believer in the idea that a dog picks you, not the other way around, and I have come to believe that,

somewhere in Diane's subconscious, she knew what was coming and picked the dog sent to be the rock that both and Mr. Oi and I were going to need.

Miss Ey is, without a doubt, the most attentive, loving creature I have ever known, and had a way of looking at you that just conveyed love and hope. It has also become significant to me that Ey was born on the 5th of August, 2008 and Diane was to pass on the 5th of August, 2009.

————————◆

When I walked in that evening, Di was laying on the sofa, clearly having taken a nap but thankfully slur-free. Maybe the night out was still an option. That thought didn't last long though, as it became obvious that she was still down about her parents leaving.

The conversation hit an old theme almost immediately; she hated it here, hated her job, and wanted to move back to South Carolina.

Now, the frustrating thing for me was that she always went down that route when drinking or angry, and yet I had agreed to move back, quit my job as soon as I found another, and we had even both agreed that we would save up and move back to England, where Diane was at her happiest.

Despite this, here we were again going over the same pointless argument that would either see us not talking or her drinking and emailing or texting family and old work colleagues about how she hated it here, and if she could get her old job back in the Sheriff's Department– none of which she had any intention of doing.

This was proven by the fact she'd insisted we buy the house we had just moved into and expressed her love of the area and weather multiple times. I had tried support; I had tried love and now I was fed up. It had been a long day, and unknown to me at this stage, I was carrying baggage from my childhood that was triggered by actions that made me feel inadequate. I hated my job as much as she did and I didn't need this right now, so I decided maybe tough love would work. I told her she needed to get a grip and stop with the pity party as it was wearing thin.

Di looked at me from the sofa, and said, "You have no idea how close I am to ending this!" I immediately took this as a threat to leave me, a threat I had heard many times over the last year, every time she got drunk and a threat I knew she withdrew as soon as she sobered up. It was also only the week before that she sent me a text, saying, "Please listen to Pink's song *Please Don't Leave Me*, it's me and I am so sorry. Just don't give up on me."

I had listened to the song, and, in truth, it truly could have been written for the last year of our lives together. I loved that girl with all my heart, and there was no way I would ever have given up or left her. It's not who I am.

So, it pissed me off to be back there again, and I told her, "You do whatever you think is right!" and that I was going to watch the military channel in the other room.

I have spent many hours contemplating those words since that night, how to me it was clear she was attacking me again with threats of leaving. The thought that she meant anything else never entered my mind.

Why would it? She hadn't said or done anything to suggest suicide before, and yet I was to find out, long after my knowing would have made a difference, that she had mentioned it and attempted it before and, somehow, nobody thought it wise to tell me.

Now, don't get me wrong, I was no angel in all this, and reflection does allow an objective look at yourself and for many reasons, some realisations were to come to the surface nine years later. I could have been a much better husband than I was. I could have done so much more if I had not let my issues cloud my judgement or let the soldier in me convince me that I needed to take the lead as she was not able.

I had reached out to her family at one point and explained my fears of her potential drink and drugs problem. I asked for help as I realised I was fast becoming overwhelmed. I was laughed at and told to stop exaggerating. I should have sought professional help but was too worried about what people would say about her, about us, and so decided the soldier in me was strong enough to cope. I trusted that it would all work itself out.

The nights she got drunk, angry, and tried to drive off; normally prevented by me snatching the keys, resulting in me being punched, or blocking her off when she had the keys so she couldn't get in the car.

One night, she beat me to the keys and the car, and my only hope was to stand in the drive in front of the car, which resulted in Diane driving at me, flipping me over the hood and dumping me on the curb. Luckily, that worked, and she got out and came back to make sure I was ok. I was ok, bruised, but ok. I comforted her, parked the car and took her gently back into the house. The bruises were worth stopping her from driving away and ruining her life if pulled over, or worse, killing herself or someone else.

There were nights I sat up watching her, fearing she would vomit and choke, too unconscious to wake up. The mixture of drinks would leave her passed out, and I remember waking one night to find the bed soaking wet, realising she had wet the bed. I was furious! I got up, went to the spare room and got into bed. I stayed there for about 20 minutes before I realised that, if she woke and I was not there, she would be deeply embarrassed, and so I went back, grabbed a towel, rolled her onto it and got back into bed. When the alarm went off, she looked at what was under her, immediately knew, and in silence headed for the shower. I got up, stripped the bed and put it in the laundry. When she came out of the shower, she looked at the stripped bed, said nothing but hugged me like there was no tomorrow. That became our routine for such events.

Well, I found out that I wasn't strong enough and it didn't work itself out. I am forever haunted by the fear of what she heard me say that night. I am haunted by the idea that instead of hearing me say "leave me if you have to," she heard, "end your life if you have to." I live in the fear that she saw her one true rock turn his back on her. It hurts me beyond words to think that she felt I was going to leave her and that my words pushed her deeper into the Dark. I failed her.

———————◆

About an hour or so later, I'm not clear on the precise timeline, I could hear her talking on the phone and so I decided to tentatively test our proven "not mad anymore" test.

Whenever we argued in the past, one of us would always test the water by either saying, "I'm having a beer, do you want one?" If the answer was yes, we both knew that the argument was over and we could get back to "Happyville." Alternatively, if you really weren't sure, one of us would just grab two beers from the fridge, open them both and from a safe angle offer the other one the second beer. If it was accepted, bingo, fight over! If it was rejected, however, the fight was still on but at least you now had two beers! I didn't want to interrupt her on the phone, so I raised the bottle so she could see it and she beckoned for me to pass it over to her... Success!

I quietly whispered to her, asking who she was talking to, and she mouthed to me through the conversation that it was the mother of a girl she was teaching to ride who was planning on buying her spare saddle the following day. I gave her a quick thumbs up and told her I was going to finish watching my program and would then be back to join her. She shot me a quick smile and nodded. As I walked away, relieved and happy, I heard her arranging to meet the woman the following day for coffee to complete the sale.

I have no idea what happened between that moment of reconciliation and hearing the shot, but forensics showed both a sleeping drug, in the vein of Ambien, and alcohol in her system. I can only assume that she had decided to make today end in the hope that tomorrow would be a better day as she had so many times before, and that she hoped to achieve this by taking a sleeping pill washed down with a mini bottle of vodka and taking herself off to bed. It was the sleeping pill, not the vodka, that made her slur and gave the game away to me.

I had found out a few years before that Ambien had a very distinct and fast-acting effect on Diane, to the point it scared me. In response, I'd thrown away her tablets and strongly warned her not to get more. Unbeknownst to me, in the US, a doctor will give a prescription that includes several refills, so all she did was refill it and hide them. In the UK you have to get a new prescription for every refill, so this never occurred to me. My guess is that she took both the drug and the mini bottle, as her actions and the way the tablets affected her led to the worst moment of my life...

Urgency, Hope, and Loss

The following chapter contains graphic descriptions of suicide and its aftermath. I urge you to think carefully about the decision to read the following chapter. If at any stage you feel like you cannot continue, put down the book and take some time for yourself. When you return, if you feel unable then read on, or you would not like to read this chapter at all, move on to the following chapter.

An immediate scan of the room revealed nothing. Could I have been wrong? The shot sounded like it came from the master bedroom? I was mid-turn, about to take off for the living room when my peripheral vision caught movement, and I turned to see Mr. Oi, ears down, licking at something with Miss Ey on the other side of whatever it was. Our room had the main bed central with a large dressing table unit, complete with a large mirror, to its right. This was Diane's side of the bed, which only left about three feet of space and not enough room for much. What were they so intently focused on? My mind racing, I shouted for them to move and as they did, I saw Diane's legs, folded underneath her and her body slumped against the bed.

I heard myself shout, "Diane what have you done!?"

I could now see the wound under her chin and an ever-widening pool of blood staining the sheets and covering the floor underneath her, her Glock pistol at her side. For what seemed a lifetime, I stood and absorbed the image, trying to make sense of it all, rapidly taking in and making sense of every detail. In reality, it was seconds before my training kicked in and I started making assessments and decisions based on that training. I knew that if I was to save her, I had to move her as there was not nearly enough room where she had fallen. I instinctively grabbed her shirt and dragged her across the floor to the end of the bed. I felt strangely vacant. I couldn't think straight, like it wasn't happening, or at any moment she was going to laugh at me, and it was all a big joke. She always played jokes on me, surely this had to be another...

But I also knew it wasn't. That was just me trying to shut out reality. A coping mechanism that came immediately into action. As I looked down at her, something in my head screamed, "breathing, bleeding, breaks and burns!" The phrase, drummed into me during military team medic training, brought me sharply to awareness and knew I had to get her to breathe.

Kneeling next to her, I cupped her head and pushed two fingers into her mouth, knowing that wound debris could be blocking her airway. She seemed dead, but I had to try, I couldn't give her up without a fight, and as I reached down her mouth I hooked tissue and something - possibly bone - out of her throat and she suddenly took in an immense, rasping gasp of air and kicked back into me.

"Fight Diane, Fight! Don't you dare give up on me!"

The wave of hope that washed over me was almost overwhelming and for a second, I believed it was all going to be ok, but my training told me reality doesn't care much for hope and I became aware that the roof of her mouth was missing when I had cleared her airway. She was far from out of danger.

I needed help and I needed it fast! My phone was in the other room... fuck it! I had no choice, I had to lay her down and get my phone. As I bolted to the spare room, Oi and Ey followed me– I assumed later that my panicked run made them feel that there was danger so they followed to protect me. This helped; I knew I had to lock them away before help arrived in case Oi became protective and got himself shot as well.

I locked them both in the spare room and ran - phone in hand - back to Diane. Weeks later, I read a copy of the Police report that included the transcripts and reports of all those involved. I was shocked to read that the 911 dispatcher stated that she was unsure at first if I was male or female because I sounded so hysterical, and yet inwardly I felt calm and in control, that I was following drills, but I guess on the outside I was desperate for someone to get there and help me. The reason we train over and over in the military is precisely so that even when we lose control, we still function as trained.

I remember telling myself, "You must stop or slow the bleeding" as the realisation dawned on me that I was covered in her blood, and while the entry wound was obvious, the exit wound was not where I expected it to be, and I started to panic. I expected the wound to be large and easy to find somewhere around the back of her head and it just wasn't there. Where the fuck was it!? I had to find it! I now know the shot had gone straight up, an angle I hadn't considered, and was actually quite small because of the speed and limited travel distance of the bullet and was concealed by her fringe (bangs to Americans), and I missed it completely.

I'd put my phone on the end of the bed on loudspeaker because I needed both hands and was vaguely aware of questions coming from the lady at dispatch, but all I could think was, "where the fuck are they!?" The Fire Department, and hence AMS, was less than five minutes from my house and I remember yelling, "Hurry the fuck up...where the fuck are they!?"

I worried that this time was going to cost me Diane and looked at what I could do to save time. To save her. Every second mattered, every action buying the precious time she needed. I laid her back down and I sprinted to the front door, opened it, and ran back. Logic told me that this would allow them to come straight in when they arrived, and I wouldn't have to leave her alone. Logic and training. Fix the problem, buy time. Buy back some of the time that she had lost so much blood that was not forming a second puddle at the foot of the bed.

These two puddles of blood now covered the floor, smeared by a combination of me dragging Di to where she was now and me, now sitting on the

51

floor with her. As I sat on the floor, freshly wet, I pulled her up into my arms, her back to my chest, head laid back onto my shoulder and wrapped my arms around her while I held a shirt against her chin, thinking that even though I couldn't find the exit wound, I knew that by elevating her I could slow the flow of blood.

It was at this moment, cradling my dying wife in my arms, with the situation at its most bleak, that I felt a pang of hope as she started to moan and very deliberately lifted one foot at a time, placing them flat on the bedroom floor and, when both were set, she pushed up with her legs as if trying to stand. I felt a surge of love and pride. My wife, my Diane, a fighter, fighting this with every bit of strength she had left.

This convinced me that it had to have been an accident. But how!? She tried to push herself up several times. I knew that this would only speed up the process of blood loss, that her strength and determination to fight would only make her weaker.

I had to calm her down, reassure her that the situation was under control, "Stop trying, I've got you, they're on their way. Stop moving, but don't you dare quit on me! You told me not to quit on you so don't you dare quit on me now! Fight Diane, fight! Don't you dare leave me, I love you and I cannot lose you! Fight! Please, please, fight babe…"

What followed was the longest wait of my life. 12 agonising minutes to be precise, with every second feeling like an hour as, despite my calm reassurances to Diane, the fear of her slipping away occupied my every thought. Finally, after 12 excruciatingly long minutes, I heard the shout from my door from the first police officer to arrive. My training served me well once again. I knew from experience that the first concern for the officer was going to be that a gun had been fired, somebody had been shot, and he needed to know where that gun was. Subconsciously aware of this, I had already shoved the pistol across the floor away from us when I first dragged her, partly because I knew what to expect and partly out of anger at the gun.

"In here, in here! Hurry up!"

My chest heaved with a sudden rush of anxiety at their lack of urgency, but on reflection, I know that they couldn't simply take my word for it and blunder into what could have been a trap. I have to say at this point that the officers of Surprise PD and the Surprise AMS were outstanding, even though at the time I may not have expressed that. My hat is well and truly off to you. My respect and my admiration are sincere.

Again, on reflection I understand, but I was still surprised to see an officer, gun drawn, enter my bedroom. His first words were, "Where is the gun?"

"There, you fucking wanker!" I shouted pointing frantically at the gun before asking, "Where the fuck are the paramedics!?"

It was at this stage that the paramedics forced their way into the room, ignoring the officer who had told them to stay at the front door until he cleared the house. Having heard me and the frantic tone of my voice, they made the decision to press on with trying to save whoever was injured. They gently, but firmly and with control, lifted her away from me and laid her on the floor where they proceeded to work on her. They asked me for her name and what had happened to her, and I believe I gave them as detailed a report as I could - my training again - but to be brutally honest, I'm not entirely sure what I said.

The officer had by now holstered his firearm and ushered me out of the room into the corridor, promising me that we would leave the door open so I could see her. If I'm honest, I don't actually remember much about what he asked me or said to me. My brain has locked away parts of that night, as it has big chunks of the next few years, somewhere deep in my head, probably for my own good. What I do remember, and will always stick with me, was his kindness as he asked me tough questions, fully aware that I was watching the love of my life fight for her life.

Other officers arrived, more paramedics, and I heard a paramedic say, "Stop Diane, stop. Lay still, we got you." She'd carried on fighting, and I remember allowing a slight feeling of hope to enter my mind as I mentally willed her on with every ounce of my being. Shortly after, a paramedic briefly came out of the room and told me that they had managed to get her blood pressure back up to a more stable level and, while she was very seriously hurt, she was fighting and the situation looked more promising. He also told me that the air ambulance was about to land, kindling my hope even further.

———————◆

The thing about Hope is, it's a blessing, one that gives you strength and willpower. But it's also a right bastard. Hope will pull you through the darkest times, convincing you that there's a light at the end of the tunnel. It will give you the strength that you need at the time that you most need it. Hope can convince you that the odds are in your favour, even when they are overwhelmingly not. It overrides logic.

Hope can convince you that everything will turn out ok, that every little positive sign or moment will swing the pendulum in your favour and give you everything you want or need. Hope gave me the strength to help my wife as she lay dying on our bedroom floor. Hope and training. Hope convinced me that she would make it out of this alive, that she would emerge from the other side of this and, despite our lives irrevocably changing, we would go on loving each other.

Losing Hope is a death sentence within itself, a fact that all sufferers of PTSI know only too well. Hope can damage us in many ways. A life without Hope is an empty life, one without optimism or satisfaction, without the sense that great things are destined to come your way. The Darkness thrives where there is no Hope. Hope is light, a way through the pain, and the Darkness hates that. In my experience, the only thing worse than having no Hope to begin with, is having Hope, allowing that Hope to convince you that everything is going to be ok before reality brings to life the very thing that Hope convinced you would never happen. That empty, shattered feeling you are left with is the ultimate sense of betrayal. It's hard to trust again after that. It's hard to trust people, circumstances…anything. This lack of trust turns to hatred, rage, despair, and you dare not let yourself Hope again. This is the hardest thing to overcome, your lack of trust in Hope. One of the biggest lessons I've had to teach myself is that it's ok to Hope. But here, with what happened next, I abandoned all Hope, for many long years.

———————————◆

The officer told me I couldn't go on the flight– the chopper was too small for that. I knew inside that they were still trying to determine whether or not I was the shooter. I can remember snarling at an officer that I was going with my wife and warning him not to get in my way.

An older officer, I want to say a Sgt, but I'm not sure, read my mind and said, "Mark, if we thought it was you, you'd already be in cuffs. We have a car to take you, but you can't go on the chopper. Now, how about you change your shirt quick and wash up a bit?"

I looked down as his eyes dropped to my shirt and for the first time realised how much blood was on my shirt and hands. It felt surreal, washing my wife's blood from my hands and face as I could hear them getting her ready to wheel out to the helicopter. It was surreal in the sense that it felt as if it was all a dream, a show that I was watching, and that it would all be over soon. She would be home again safe. Hope.

But the reality was I just watched them wheel my wife past me and out the front door, watched as they loaded her onto the helicopter and lifted off into the night sky. I had seen helicopters lift off before with wounded or injured on board, but never my wife.

That was the last time I would see my wife alive.

She Didn't Make it...

It seemed like an eternity before the car was ready to take me, but the senior officer asked me if I had anyone to call who could meet me at the hospital. I had no family in Arizona, so I called two friends and asked them to meet me at the hospital, telling them only that Diane had shot herself.

I was led to a minibus and handed over to a male and female welfare officer team who would be my lift to the hospital. Before I left, the officer told me to stay strong and that he would pray for Diane. I welled up, my walls dropping and asked him to take care of the pups and not let anyone hurt them, they were just stressed. He promised me he would, and he kept his word. He sat with them and gave them dinner before he left. I was on my way to the hospital.

I remember feeling frustrated, pissed off at the driver because he drove the speed limit the entire way, We lived on the Western edge of the Phoenix valley, so it took almost an hour for us to reach the major trauma hospital in downtown Phoenix. I knew that he had to do his job and obey the law like anyone else, but I didn't care, and I was getting more and more stressed, stressed to the point of complaining.

We were about halfway down AZ State 303 towards the I10 Interstate when my mind went silent. I felt a deep sensation engulf my entire body, tingling, warm, and somehow comforting. My stress at the driver, the evening, drained away and I felt an inner calm, a peacefulness almost, an acceptance.

I knew at that moment that she was gone. I knew she had come to say goodbye and ease my pain.

I looked at my watch and it later turned out to be the recorded time of her passing. The rest of the drive passed by in silence, and I found myself stunned, a million thoughts racing through my mind, all at once. No answers, just questions. And shock. Shock at how just over two hours ago, my only thoughts were about tomorrow and how maybe we could go out for dinner. Now, tomorrow was gone. Everything was gone, and while a glimmer of hope struggled to make itself seen, to deny the truth, I knew - I could feel - that she was gone. I was alone and every dream, plan or hope I had was now gone.

The look on the receptionist's face when she read the screen after being asked where Mrs. Spicer was told me all I needed to know. She did her best, bless her, to hide the look in a false hope of somehow saving me from the pain for a bit longer. But it was too late, I'd seen it.

When we arrived at the family room my friends Ryan and Dave were already there, and their clear discomfort confirmed that any last hope was a waste of time. Dave was a police officer and so I knew he would have used that to get me any news he could when he arrived, so I directed my question at him.

"Any news?" His hesitation was cut by my second question, "She didn't make it did she?"

He shook his head and told me she'd survived the flight and they lost her just after she arrived at the OR. Now, Ryan was a little upset at Dave for telling me. he thought it may have come better from the Doctor, but I was grateful to Dave, and I still am to this day, for being honest and knowing I wouldn't want to be kept in the dark, holding onto false hope and that it was best to just tell me. It was a brave and compassionate action– the action of a true friend.

In the downward spiral that followed, I was to alienate Dave with my behaviour as I struggled to come to terms with that night, as I did several other friends. Now, that isn't an excuse, and I take full blame for it, it is merely me explaining that I now know why I acted as I did. So to Dave and anyone else I pushed away, insulted or hurt, I am truly sorry.

My immediate thought at Dave's admission was; what if she gave up because she couldn't hear me anymore? What if, somewhere deep in her subconscious, she thought I had given up on her and stopped fighting? I should have insisted on going with her.

I guess I now realise that her injuries were just too severe, and a few days later I spoke with one of the paramedics from that night, who told me he'd never seen anyone fight so hard and that, considering her injuries, they couldn't believe she kept trying to stand or even regained a form of consciousness. I feel immense pride at being able to say that about her.

He also told me that the damage to her brain would have meant she would never have been the girl I knew and loved again and that it was probably better she passed. That helped me come to terms a little bit and was a kind gesture, but my own struggles were only just beginning.

I was upset that they wouldn't let me see her and no matter how much they tried to explain that in a suicide or gun death her body was now evidence and that nobody was allowed near her except the Coroner, I didn't get it. I wouldn't accept it.

I do now, but at the time I desperately needed to see her, and this wounded me profoundly. Ryan and Dave did their best to calm and comfort me, but it was my years of training that allowed me to function and not fall to the ground as I wanted. I became agitated at one of the hospital administration staff who was overly pushy about who my medical insurance was with. I was frustrated that I had not had the presence of mind to bring it with me and before I lost my temper with her, Dave stepped in, telling her to come back later and to try and find her compassion while she was at it, and I remember a small moment of mirth at Dave's sarcasm in my defence.

A short time later, I excused myself. I poignantly remember this moment. It was the first time I experienced a feeling that would come to define me over the following years whenever I felt overwhelmed with anxiety. I felt closed in. I needed space. I walked myself outside and paced, up and down, oblivious to time and the world, with thought after thought bouncing around inside my head, not knowing what to do.

At some point, the realisation, and the dread, came to me that I would have to tell Diane's parents and family - my family - that Diane had gone. Nausea rushed through me, and I gagged as I nearly threw up. I didn't, a couple of deep breaths brought calm back to my stomach and I considered how best to pass this on to people; her mum and dad who, hours ago, had been here with her and whom I knew were going to blame themselves.

Diane had all but begged them to stay a few more days and they had said no. Normally a predictable and legitimate answer, but, given the current news, an answer that they would now second guess for the rest of their lives.

Diane's older sister was a paramedic and so my garbled mind reasoned that she would be strong, and it would be best if she was with them when I told them, or if I told her and she told them. So, I called her first. I guess life has a way of making you do the right thing even when you don't want to, and inside, a part of me knew that my decision was partly one of avoiding responsibility by asking Denise to tell her parents. She didn't answer, and I later found out she had changed phones so I couldn't have gotten through to her anyway. I also realised Denise was probably not going to be in a fit state to do it either and this was, and had to be, my responsibility.

A Trauma Shared

After dialling the number to Roosevelt's phone and pausing before dialling the final number several times, I hit send and listened as it started to ring. I knew that the time difference meant it was the early hours of the morning in South Carolina and I thought, or hoped, I guess, that maybe he wouldn't answer. But he did.

"Hey Roosevelt, sorry to wake you, I know you haven't been home long. Is Betty with you?"

"Yep, she's right here. Everything ok?"

The next words are probably the hardest I have ever had to say in my life. He had me on speakerphone, so I heard Betty's grief pour out of her when I told them, and it cut me to the core. Roosevelt was the southern gentleman I had come to know and love. He embodied a calmness I admire to this day. He thanked me for calling and asked if I was going to be ok, said sorry that I was alone out there and told me to stay strong. I couldn't speak as I simply stood there. Tears streamed down my face as we ended the call.

Diane was one of those people it was almost impossible not to love. Those that didn't love her often hated her– it was easy to be jealous of her. On the whole, though, she was a burst of sunshine with a wicked sense of humour and an infectious laugh. Many times, children from a former marriage don't take to a woman who comes into their dad's life, but my son and my daughter had both taken to her and developed deeply personal relationships, maybe not at first, but were now well and truly family with her.

Next, I needed the support only a mother could give, so I called my mum. She immediately offered to remove some of the stress by offering to tell my kids. I thanked her but said it had to come from me.

My son has always been a strong character, tremendously caring and supportive of others, but I knew it hurt, especially as he had visited us with my mum not so long back and his memories of Diane were fresh.

My daughter was a police officer back in the UK and so had a lot in common with Diane. They often joked and told stories to each other, and I knew she was on the night shift and so she was awake. I composed myself and called her phone. She answered and I gave some piss-poor excuse as to why I had called and asked what she was up to.

She told me she was on a mobile vehicle patrol with her Sgt, which allowed me to jokingly ask her to put him on. After giving me a stern warning not to embarrass her, she passed him the phone. Knowing that he would be able to offer some support that physically I could not, I told him to act normal and that I was about to give Gemma some very bad news, asking him to look after her. He said he would and not to worry in a way that sounded like we had just had a laugh about something and gave her the phone back. He came back on the phone a few minutes after I broke the news to her and told me he was taking her home and not to worry. I thanked him and hung up.

I was almost in machine-mode, calm, calculated, calling family to tell them and, with the exception of when I spoke to family, I shed very few tears. With this done, I remembered the dogs left at home, our dogs, and in the absence of being able to see my wife, felt an overwhelming urge to go home and make sure the pups were ok. I owed it to her.

Dave and Ryan both tried to talk me out of going back to the house, but I had to. Something was pulling at me and so I told them they either drove me or I would fucking walk. They drove me and stayed for an hour or so until the awkward silence was more painful than being alone and I sent them both home. They had been up most of the night with me and I knew they were both tired and, to be honest, I wanted to be alone.

The pups were stressed. Oi wouldn't leave my side and Ey had taken to hiding. I was numb. The need to be outside came back and I walked out to the front of my house and sat with my back to a tree, looking at my empty house. Dawn was breaking and the sun was just coming up over the horizon. The front of my house lit up as the first rays of a new day fell across it, and, where normally I would have felt lucky to have the life I had, with a beautiful wife and an amazing house, I remember thinking to myself; how did a home become just a house so quickly. The pain of this thought broke me, and I finally broke down and cried as I'd never cried before.

I'm not sure how long I cried for or what time I went back into the house but when I did, I was numb.

Not long before Diane's passing, I'd become very good friends with another sniper and career operator who was due to leave the service and come work with me at the training school I headed. Our families had become friends and so, when I called him at daybreak the morning after her suicide, he got straight in his car and immediately drove to Phoenix from San Diego to be with me.

Our dogs had taken their Momma's death as bad as I had, Mr. Oi in particular, who had taken to swimming in the pool to the point of exhaustion, almost as if in an attempt to drown or punish himself. I was so concerned at his repeated actions that I bought dog life-vests and they had to wear them any time they were near the pool. I read in later years that studies have shown that dogs grieve in much the same way humans do, which has been evidenced by the fact that all the same parts of a dog's brain light up as they do in a human  grieving, so I have no doubts that Mr. Oi suffered greatly at losing the only mum he had known since birth, and who chose him because he was the runt of the litter.

Diane's mum and oldest sister had flown out the next day, followed by two mates over the next few weeks from the UK; one even gave up his job to do so, and so Chris, Bry and Rob became my caretakers. The following days passed in a haze; hours sat in the living room without anyone saying a word.

Eventually, almost a week later, we were allowed to visit the Chapel of Rest and see her. I had been asked to provide clothing for her to be buried in, and so I'd sent her favourite outfit days before. It was surreal to see her laying there, dressed as I had seen her on a night out only days ago, motionless and still, heavily made up to conceal the paleness caused by the lack of blood flow, and so when I reached for her hand, it came as a sharp shock to feel the cold of her hand. I sobbed. She wasn't there.

Her mum and sister were amazing help and very supportive of me, unlike several members of her family who would show their true colours at her funeral a week later. At the Chapel of Rest, I found myself ready to seriously hurt the overbearing Chapel Manager and test the limits of his medical insurance, who pestered and refused to give Betty time alone with her daughter. Initially, my anger was stopped by Rob, but even he looked like he was going to cause the man harm until he eventually returned to his office and allowed us space.

After leaving, and on the drive home, we were passing a bar when Betty said, "You know what Mark, I think we all need a drink!" This drew a small chuckle from all of us, and so we stopped and grabbed a table. We probably had two drinks each in total silence, with a server who must have wondered what the hell our issue was, and then we paid and headed to the house, to sit in further silence, interspersed with someone quietly sobbing while the rest knew to just let it happen.

The next few days saw me busy learning what I had to do to take Diane home to South Carolina for her funeral, all the while knowing a fight was coming. Diane and I had spoken often about our wishes after death, and she was most adamant about what she wanted if she passed first, something that on reflection, she knew was probably her plan. Diane was insistent that she be cremated, and her ashes stayed with me and the pups. She didn't want to be left in South Carolina and miss all the fun and made me give her my word.

I have broken many promises in my life, to my shame, but I have never broken my word, and she knew that, so she was decidedly insistent on the wording of my sentence. I knew that it was not going to go well with her family, a deeply southern family who expected her to be buried near them, and I was not mistaken.

Betty was the first I broached the subject with, and to my surprise, she said I was her husband and that it was my decision. It came to a head a few days later when a phone call from her dad explained all the arrangements they had made for the funeral, including my sister-in-law who, in true good spirit, was arranging for a rolling picture presentation to run throughout the ceremony. When Betty said, "I think you all need to slow down and ask Mark," the trouble started. Roosevelt was hurt, I could hear it in his voice. He was, however, a man of principles and a very kind man, and so he agreed and deferred to my, and Diane's, wishes. Not all of the family agreed.

On the day we took her home I briefed Chris, who was my pup-sitter, that if any of my pups drowned, I would tell his unit he was a failure, and with that small attempt at humour, we headed to the airport. The funeral home took her to the airport and just called me to update me on the movements. It was at the gate that I realised I couldn't see the aircraft hold doors and I felt a surge of emotional panic build.

I had to make sure she was ok and on the plane. Barely holding back tears, I explained to the customer service rep my issue, and she very kindly escorted me into their staff lounge that overlooked my plane and told me I could sit there as long as I wanted. That moment of kindness has stayed with me, along with similar acts on our flights home.

The flight was painfully long and the drive to Greenville from Charlotte was no better. Walking into the family home was hard without Diane, made harder by some of the family who clearly had an issue with me.

One thing Diane did, which hurts me to this day, was when she was on Ambien or vodka, she would indulge her habit of calling family or old work bosses and telling them how she hated Arizona, she hated me and wanted to come back. In truth, we had this conversation multiple times to which I offered to give what she seemed to be asking for, but when sober, she would insist she didn't want to and even forced my hand into buying a house.

To a family who never witnessed the morning after, I can see the questions, it hurts, but I can see why they felt the way they did. To me, that was a huge attack on my character and my love for her, and for the first time I found myself thinking; what if they think I did it?

It came to a head over the next few days when Betty had finally had enough and called everybody out on their attitudes. She explained what she and Denise saw over the first few days, how broken I was, and how my love for Diane was without question, and anyone who was going to be harsh and unkind to me needed to stay away from her house. It meant a lot to me, but the mere thought that someone thought I would do that played on my mind and hurt me in the worst way.

A tradition in South Carolina is that the night before a funeral, the family and friends would come to the Chapel and pay their respects to the deceased and say goodbye. It was normally an open-coffin affair and the thought of standing there for hours looking at my wife filled me with such dread and anxiety that I doubted my ability to sit through and endure it.

On the day before Diane's funeral, an hour before the first guests were due to arrive, the funeral director, a very kind and compassionate man, called me to one side. He explained to me that, because of the delay in funeral caused by her autopsy and the travel arrangements, the make-up that had been applied was not fully concealing the changes in colour or skin texture. He suggested that we close the coffin.

I knew that this was going to down like a lead balloon, but I also remembered something Diane had said in jest before; "If I die first, you shut the lid and don't give my enemies any chance of a last laugh at me." So, I compromised and told him I wouldn't close it until her parents and siblings had said goodbye, but that it was to be closed before any guests arrived. I was thankful and relieved when her parents and family agreed.

Standing there, even with the coffin closed, was a very traumatic event for me. I'm sure it is for anybody that has lost a wife or a husband, but the unexpected and sudden way I lost her still hadn't sunk in, and the images of the way she died refused to leave my mind.

My mum and my son had flown over for the funeral from the UK. So had Donel and Ricky, two police officers from Northern Ireland whom I had known for years from deployments, and the two men instrumental in me and Diane meeting in Kosovo. Their arrival lifted my spirits and gave me a much-needed boost, reminding me of a better time and not the fucking images of my wife as she died. Ricky, Donel, Jeff & Dani, Jason & Wendy and Greg, close friends from Greenville, all went out of their way to support me, and it brings me shame to admit that I probably upset or let each of them down over the next five years as I struggled to come to terms with what happened. You'll hear me say this over and over, and yet it will never be enough– I am truly, very sorry.

Diane's suicide was not the first I'd witnessed at close range. Back in the early days of my career, I watched a friend take his own life. Maybe that had helped prepare me for what life now had in store.

The day of the funeral was difficult. That sounds obvious, but even for someone as operationally-minded and regimented as I am, it was tough. The Greenville Sheriff had agreed to bury Diane as an officer, even though she had retired.

Throughout my career, it was always me handing the folded flag to the families of the fallen, so it was surreal to be handed a folded flag. I now understood, truly, what it meant to the parents, husbands and wives of those for whom I had done the same. I will always be thankful for that mark of respect shown towards her and her love of being an officer. It provided a small amount of comfort on an otherwise awful day.

I was emotionally spent, numb, as I collected her ashes. This numbness stayed with me for a long time after Diane's funeral. My friends did their best to lift my mood, but I was already spiralling out of control and denying it publicly, as I would for the next decade. My mind was already forming my "plan."

My mum and son flew ahead of me to Phoenix, where the ever-loyal Chris picked them up and took them shopping before heading back to San Diego. I followed a few days later after Betty asked me to stay a while longer. I think that for Betty, saying goodbye to me was saying a final goodbye to Diane.

At the airport, I suddenly realised there was another issue. My boarding group was group 7 and so there was likely going to be no overhead space left. I knew that if somebody tried to take her ashes away from me, there was going to be violence.

I approached the desk when it was quiet and explained to the woman my concerns. She reassured me, telling me not to worry. That was when she called First Class and told me to go ahead and board. With immense relief, I boarded my first flight.

While waiting for my second, flight the desk attendant called my name and when I got to the desk, she told me that the attendant from Greenville had called her and explained my situation and to board when she called my name next. I boarded my second flight with the crew. The only issue I had taking her home was the TSA muppet who, as I approached him to ask for directions, screamed at me to back up. I explained I just wanted to ask a question, but he persisted in shouting across the airport at me, and even at two in the morning, it drew everyone's attention. I remember shouting back at him that if he shouted at me again, I would knock him the fuck out, turning and walking away, ignoring his calls to stop where I was. I know he was doing his job, but maybe they need a bigger budget and some training.

I have spent many hours considering my life, thinking over what had happened and why. I couldn't ignore the fact that some blamed me for what happened to Diane, and so I ran and reran both our lives and that night through my head over and over again.

While I concluded that I could have been a better husband, I felt a degree of reassuring certainty that it was not my fault, and the fact that Diane found an insurance policy that paid out even in the event of suicide would have been a red flag had I known about it.

The Surprise PD detectives were surprisingly supportive in their manner, even when they had to ask difficult questions of me. I remember the detective looking concerned when he said he had to ask me when I had last handled firearms prior to her suicide, as the swabs taken on the night had a lot of gunpowder residue on them. I explained to him that I had just finished a desert training period with soldiers of 3rd Group Special Forces and that I had picked the gun up and chucked it away from her that night. This more than compensated and he was reassuring, but it was a real fear for a while as there were no witnesses, and my mind was drawn back to the fact that people were perhaps thinking that I may have shot her and that I was responsible for her death.

Now, it has to be said that, Brit or American - I am now proudly both - means the brother/sisterhood of soldiers remains the same, and although I had only known them for a week, the guys of 3rd Group all called me when they found out and offered any help they could give– a touching gesture and I am proud to call them all now long-term friends. They truly lived up to the mantra of "Fighting soldiers from the sky" and the loyalty of the Green Beret. Thank you, gentleman.

As it turned out, forensics confirmed everyone's suspicions that, on the night, Diane had been influenced by meds and alcohol and she had suffered what they called a "one of these days" moment, where depressed, she picked up her Glock, and looking in the mirror had swung the gun up under her chin to look at the image in the mirror.

The problem was that the combination of looking in a mirror, and the effects of the chemicals in her system meant she got the distance and speed wrong and instead of just placing the gun under her chin, she slammed it, forcing the gun to violently stop and her hand to tighten, bringing her trigger finger towards her fist and firing the gun. The Glock muzzle-shaped bruise under her chin and ballistics proved the rest. To this day I do not know if I am happy that it was a tragic mistake or whether I'm angry at her.

My plan was to put my affairs in order and follow her. I gave myself a timeline, researched what had to be done to not leave my family and friends out of pocket and I adopted a fake persona, as I knew everyone was watching me like a hawk. Now, I have to point out that PTSI was a major player in this so-called plan, and while it seemed logical and the only option, it was, in fact, driven by pain, grief and the guilt of having let her down. I mean, why couldn't she tell me and let me help her?

The answer was because I was already suffering, as she was, from issues in my life and was in no position to do more. I got it wrong. I failed to read the signs and, after trying most of the supportive and empathetic methods to help her beat her depression, I opted for the army standard of tough love, and it backfired horribly. I will never forgive myself for the answer I gave her hours before she pulled the trigger. I've replayed the scene in my head a thousand times over, replayed the memory of her, in her rage, telling me, "You have no idea how close I am to ending it!"

I will never forgive myself for not reading the signs, connecting the dots, for perhaps selfishly assuming she meant us, our relationship, and replying, "You do whatever you think is right!" It will haunt me until the day I die, because she may have believed I had fallen out of love with her and didn't care, that perhaps I encouraged her to consider ending her life, pushing her along a path she had already started on.

A lot of people were there for me during this time, including my daughter, who took a sabbatical from her career in the police in the UK, along with my son, mum and family. There were friends who paid their own way over to be with me and many others who offered support in their own special way. There was Chris, Bry, Rob, Tony, Jo, but one man deserves a special mention; a man called Tom Irwin.

I had been friends with Tom for many years and Tom knew Diane well. I had told Tom that Diane was unhappy working for McMillan, and he had offered her the opportunity to work remotely for him and his company, Accuracy International. Diane was so stubborn she would not back down from her tormentors. When I told Tom what had happened, he was devastated and flew out to see me.

Over dinner, he told me he was sorry he had not pushed her harder to move jobs, but I explained to him that if I hadn't seen it coming, how could he have? Tom asked me what I was going to do, and I told him there was no way I could ever work for McMillan again and that I was quitting. He asked what they paid me and how I was going to pay my mortgage and bills and I told him, and that I had no idea how I would keep up and that I simply didn't care.

The following day I was informed via email that I was now a consultant for Accuracy International. What's more, they were going to pay me more than McMillan had, and knowing I was in no fit state to work, Tom paid me for seven months until Chris and I got Craft up and  running. To this day, he has refused to let me pay him back and every time I offer, he says, "what money?" Tom is an incredible businessman and human being. He has been there for me several times since and I would take a bullet for him any day.

One other person's reaction cut me to the core. My uncle Jack. A paratrooper from World War Two, he jumped on all major jumps, including Arnhem, from which he escaped and is now a spritely 83 years old. Uncle Jack took an instant liking to Diane, loudly telling me, well within her earshot, "I can see why you are marrying her mate, she's a bit of alright ain't she!"

He then noticed Di had heard it, and said, "Oh, sorry sweetheart, but you are a cracker!"

Every time we were in Portsmouth we would go visit him, tell stories and drink all day.

He would always greet me with the same phrase, "Hello Sgt Major, have a pint and a chaser with an old Corporal?" At our wedding, he was so full, he lost balance dancing with the ladies, and proceeded to take out the food table. Absolute fucking legend of a man. He always said he would visit us in the USA.

One day, shortly after Di passed, I was walking in circles, doing laps of my backyard deep in thought and tears when my phone rang. It was Uncle Jack; I only knew because his name came up. His choked sobs made his voice unrecognisable. The conversation was short.

"Alright, son… I don't… can't… terrible… why… I just can't… love you."

This only time I can remember my knees buckling and physically dropping to the floor, where I sobbed my heart out. That was to be the last time I heard his voice. He passed away a few months later.

He did visit me though. About six months later I was opening a package with several of my books in it, all pre-owned from shops all over the UK to give as gifts in business. I opened one to sign when I saw, as I opened the front cover, that someone had written in it already. Slightly annoyed, I read it and found myself in tears.

It was the book Di and I had given Uncle Jack. I recognised both of our writing and remembered writing the message to my Uncle Jack in it. I called my cousin Glen, Uncle Jack's son, and told him, to which he assured me the book was on his bookshelf. He checked, discovering it was gone and to this day we cannot explain how that book came home to me. All I know is that when I hold it, I see an image of both Di and my Uncle Jack standing together, laughing, and so I guess he came to see me after all. Uncle Jack's medals still hang proudly on my wall at home, and I am eternally grateful to Glen for allowing me the honour of keeping them safe.

My Dad

F or as long as I can remember, my dad has always been my hero. I don't remember my dad as a soldier. My older brother does, but I don't. All I know is it was who he was, and he never truly got over my mum forcing him to leave. We used to complain about having to listen to the same old story over and over, but in truth, I would pay a fortune to be able to listen to them now.

My dad was an amazing craftsman, it seemed that there was nothing he couldn't fix, build or repair and my brother is the same way. Me, I was the walking soup sandwich who could break anything, including Dad's patience and so, over time, I found myself feeling as though Dad never loved me.

My brother was good with his hands, was a good footballer like my dad had been, and they seemed to share so much more than Dad and me, and that hurt me. In truth, my dad loved me deeply and, in a recent conversation with my brother about this very topic, I found out that he saw it from completely the opposite direction, and felt that Dad had me as his favourite.

I guess asking, expressing feelings would have helped, but my dad was raised in an era where men did not display affection; they did not raise kids. Their job was to work every hour God sent to provide for their families, and so I never really had the opportunity to talk to my dad much. My mum was the go-to parent. My dad was very much the man of the house who I watched silently from across the room, always hoping he would notice me.

Speaking to my own kids, I pretty much did the same thing to them, but in my defence, my dad was my role model and I was a dad at 17. What did I know? My instinct was to copy the example given to me by my dad. On reflection, I was wrong, and I wish I had been a better father.

The memories I have of my dad are all of him being the strong silent type, but I also remember his wicked sense of humour. He was a very caring man, and I guess I never truly knew how caring until after he passed. So many of my cousins would talk about Uncle Roy always being there for them and how his passing affected so many people. My brother had always said he was going to join the army when he left school, but like many ex-soldiers, Dad tried to talk him out of it. Being an army cadet was one thing, it taught you discipline. But the regular army? No. I had always been too afraid to think about the army, and so it came as a shock to most when at 18, I joined the TAVR, the regular reserve army.

To this day I can't remember when I decided to join the reserve, but I do remember walking past two TAVR centres on my way home from college. One was almost at the college gates, and the other was on Perone Road, across the M27 motorway and near my bus stop. Each passing had me more and more interested and so, when I did join, I loved it.

I had always been interested in the military and the only toys I ever owned were toy guns, toy soldiers and a crate of Action Man/GI Joes, so I guess they really should have seen it coming. I very quickly became disillusioned with the reserve infantry. It seemed to me as uncomfortably cliquey and almost like a boy's club. Most of the JNCOs had no idea what they were doing and just shouted at or bullied their charges for the duration of the training.

On one of my weekend wars, I managed to catch the attention of the PSI, the regular army SNCO, who maintained standards and was the link to the regular Regiment your reserve unit would join in times of war. My reserve unit was attached to the Royal Hampshire Regiment - the Tigers - and the Regiment my dad had been in, and as Spicer is not a common name, I found that certain SNCOs had served with my dad as Private Soldiers, which was both a good and bad thing.

I'm not sure how I caught his attention, but I think it was when my corporal had sent me to take a message to HQ in the next forestry block, and he had seen me run the entire distance, taking note of how keen I was to do everything. He called me over and told me I was going with him on a night reconnaissance to locate the enemy!

Night vision was the stuff of movies back then and so we had to use hearing and the sense of smell to identify the enemy in the pitch black of Salisbury Plain, a long-time training area for British Forces. Creeping about in the dark, terrified that at any moment someone was going to jump me and take me prisoner was the most exciting thing I had ever done in my life, and I was hooked. Not just on soldiering, but on covert work, sneaking about and taking risks. Reconnaissance and sniping were already in my future.

As I mentioned, I was less than impressed with my Infantry unit and so I applied to attend the selection to join a specialised unit. They, with brutal honesty, advised me to stay where I was, gain some more experience and let my body develop more, as this role was very arduous. In a very typically "me" fashion, I ignored them and did it anyway.

They were right, and I got injured. However, I persevered, and I eventually joined the unit and stayed with them until I decided to join the regular army. Here, I had a solid and positive introduction to soldiering.

The men of this unit were all highly experienced and motivated. They relied on professionalism, respected everyone's role in the army and were exceedingly humble, while at the same time, having an air about them that they could, and would, tear you apart at any moment. I met some very experienced soldiers during my time in this unit, especially the regular PSIs whom all had combat experience in several combat arenas around the globe.

One of these chaps had a scar across his throat, and I suspected that someone had attempted to cut his throat. Later in life, we became friends, and I discovered when we were working together in the Middle East that my suspicions were correct. He terrified me as a young soldier, but I idolised him and wanted to be like him so bad.

Another was a Staff Sergeant everyone called Kai, a living legend of a tracker who had declined leave to stay with an indigenous tribe in the jungles of the Far East, and whom his teammates found was covered in native tattoos when they returned from leave. Kai was one of a few soldiers who had a true influence on my life. I must have displayed a certain quality during my time there, as my PSIs kept pushing me to join the regular army and I was starting to listen. At the age of 20, I took the Queen's Shilling and swore Allegiance to the Queen, Her Heirs and Successors.

Like Father, Like Son

Joining the army was a risk. I had a family to consider and a well-paying job as a vehicle technician with the Royal Mail and had just finished my apprenticeship. I would be taking a large pay cut to join the Army and would have to stick it out for three years, even if I didn't like it. Luckily, my wife agreed, and so the journey that would define and shape my life began.

I had already decided to join the Royal Hampshire Regiment: Dad's Regiment. I wanted him to be proud of me for following in his footsteps, and he was. Basic Training wasn't difficult, I had already had a fantastic introduction to soldiering and so it was no real surprise when I was awarded the Top Student prize, and I could not wait for Dad to see me receive my award on my Passing Out Parade.

The day of my Passing Out was a typical British overcast day that looked like it would turn to rain at any moment. Thankfully it didn't and feeling resplendent and important, we fell in with our Training NCOs, ready to march on the Square to the sound of the band. I think that was my first experience of an anxiety attack. I found myself struggling to breathe until we halted and faced the reviewing officer, with the families of those passing out sitting behind him. Like everyone, I searched the crowd for my family and quickly spotted them; my wife, kids. Mum and…where's my dad? I was devastated that my dad didn't come, and I immediately took it as proof that he didn't love me, confirming to me that once again I was not good enough.

I was so hurt by his absence that it took me over 30 years to ask my mum, after he had passed, why he hadn't come. Her answer typified my dad and made me remorseful of the fact that I had ever thought bad of him. Mum explained that the only car they could afford to rent wasn't big enough for all of them, so Dad stayed behind so that everyone else could go. My mum explained that he had his Regimental Tie and Blazer on and was excitedly looking forward to it but stepped back to make sure my wife and kids could be there.

Passing Out in December meant we could be used to guard the base over the Christmas period, and I soon learned that this would be common and that, in the coming years, I would miss many more family events.

During the Christmas period, as trained soldiers now, we had different accommodations and were allowed off-base when not on duty. As it turned out, the Orderly Officer and Orderly Sergeant for the holiday period were both Royal Hampshires in the last few weeks of their career. One, a huge Sergeant, said very little but was extremely intimidating. One day, as I was booking out to go shopping, the Corporal asked my name. When I replied that it was Spicer, he looked sharply up, stared at me for a few seconds, said nothing, and went back to his paper. When I returned a few hours later, he called me into the Guard Room and my heart sank.

Standing to attention before him, he said, "Is your dad Roy Spicer?" I answered that he was. He told me he knew my dad, that my dad was his Section Commander and a good bloke. He then hit me with his mallet of a fist in the solar plexus and dropped me to the Guard Room floor.

A few minutes later, when I was finally able to catch my breath, I stood up and he told me to go out back and make him a brew (cuppa tea), NATO style. I spent about 10 minutes out the back trying to work out what NATO style meant, but eventually had to go back and ask him. He called me a few choice names and told me it meant milk with two sugars, NATO Standard, in a manner that told me I was supposed to already have known that. Thankfully, he didn't drop me again for my supposed ignorance. Pete Copping, I was to find out, was a Regimental legend and truly hard man, who, if he liked you, would give you a playful slap. I was just glad he liked me, or that he liked my dad, as I would never want to have felt an angry punch from that man.

The last time I saw Pete was at the presentation of new Colours at our base in Tidworth, Hampshire, four years later. British Regiments have always had Queen's Colour and Regimental Colours - flags - though you never refer to them as anything but the Colours unless you want a broken nose. The Colours have a Regiment's battle honours embroidered on to it and it is a monumental disgrace for a unit to lose either in battle. When the Colours reach a certain age, the Regiment will stage a parade and a member of the Royal Family will present a new set, allowing the older set to be displayed in a church or cathedral. At the reception that followed the parade, I and a very good friend of mine, Bob, bumped into Pete and his wife at the bar and knocked back a few beers with them.

After a few, Pete suddenly turned on Bob with a terrifying look in his eyes and said, "Are you leering at my wife?"

My heart sank. Bob looked like he was about to have a heart attack.

"No…No, I'm not Pete!" Bob spat out, fearing they might be his last words.

"Why not, do you think she is ugly then?" The last of Bob's blood drained from his face.

At this point, Pete and his missus burst out laughing, and she calmed Bob by telling him, "Don't worry love, he does that all the time and thinks it's funny!" I have to admit, I'd already decided on my escape route and Bob's eulogy was running through my head as I was braced to be on my toes as soon as Pete locked that steam train of a fist! A true legend of a man.

With this start to my military career, I was determined to impress my dad and so gave 110% in everything I did. I desperately wanted to be promoted and make him see I was a good soldier. Promotion was also the only way you can earn more in the Army, and as my dad had instilled a drive to provide for my family in me, I also wanted promotion so I could bring in a bit more money for my family.

My first posting was to join the Battalion in Berlin, and the irony of telling my German teacher that learning German was a waste of time because I'd never use it was never more obvious. Berlin, at that time, was still deep within the communist Warsaw Pact and so your wartime role was to soak up as much punishment from the Soviet forces as you could before your eventual death. Quite an exciting prospect for a young soldier!

I loved Berlin. It took me a while to settle in and I was surprised to find out how homesick I was. I missed my wife and kids with a savage intensity, but my Platoon was a top group of blokes and one, the first to introduce himself, would go on to become a life-long friend and one of the best soldiers I've ever met.

Dane Sandford (Sandy Sandford) was actually from Southampton, and hence my hometown's life-long "enemy" in football, but whilst we abuse each other to this day, he was to become a brother to me in so many ways.

During my time in Berlin, I snapped my Fibula and Tibia (lower leg bones) playing murderball, a British Army "sport" that involved two teams, normally opposing Platoons, a full water canteen (the ball), and each side having to get a try/touchdown, similar to rugby. That's where the similarity ends. There were no other rules and punching, clotheslining, kicking, etc. were all legal. At one point, with the canteen under my arm and throwing fists at anyone who got in my way, I was rapidly closing in on the try line when Jimmy Wilmot, all four bloody feet of him, dropkicked my right shin, snapping it right through.

The injury was to put me out of action for six months, but it didn't dampen my drive and determination to advance. Once I was back on my feet, I was selected to attend a Junior Non-Commissioned Officers course (JNCO Cadre) after only being in the Army for just over a year, when 3-5 years would be the normal qualifying period. I was both ecstatic and terrified at the same time - ecstatic because I wanted to be an NCO and lead instead of following, and terrified because I wasn't sure I had enough experience… Good ol' impostor syndrome!

I wasn't worried about the fitness aspect of the class, I was fit before I joined the Army and I had a Company Sgt Major, Andy Andrews, who decided that his three platoons didn't need trucks to go the three miles to the rifle ranges. We could just run with full platoon kit and weapons. Andy was the kind of soldier young soldiers looked up to, outrageously fit and a man who knew that as much as we complained about his decision, we would be thankful in combat when it would be needed.

In 1984, full platoon kit and weapons meant each soldier running - we never walked or marched anywhere - carrying a minimum of 45lb in belt kit plus their SLR rifles, adding another 9.5lb. If that wasn't already enough, the Sections each had three Carl Gustav 84mm anti-tank weapons, weighing in at 31lb each, as well as 3 FN GPMGs as section machine guns, adding another 26lbs. These weapons always were supposed to be passed around during the run, but it's amazing how deaf soldiers can become when you're looking for someone else to take their turn, so the heavy weapons always ended up being carried by the same poor soldiers.

The physical side of the course never concerned me. It was the leadership and teaching side. The course was carefully designed to turn you into both leaders and teachers, able to administer, train and lead your men in combat. Therefore, by necessity, the course incorporated very long hours, a mass of new information and concluded with a final test exercise to confirm whether you passed, failed or had excelled.

In typical British Army fashion, the final test started with a forced march in full kit (with each man having on average 120lb on his back), the entire length of Berlin overnight, followed by a full-scale company attack on a simulated enemy position at first light. The course was gruelling, a blur at times. Sleep wasn't high on the Directing Staff's (DS) agenda. Despite the intense physical and intellectual challenges, it was oddly enjoyable. It's hard to explain just how funny it is seeing your mate get beasted by the DS, or falling over because he is so tired when you yourself are exhausted. When you are that tired, everything is hilarious and once you start laughing you just can't stop! There were many occasions where we'd all be hysterically laughing for 15 minutes, and by the end, nobody could remember what actually started it!

The other situation guaranteed to get you into trouble with the DS for laughing was in our classroom lessons. On occasion, the students were required to run lessons to prove we had both the knowledge and confidence to face a group and teach in a composed, confident and structured manner.

As anyone who knows will tell you, when teaching it is all too easy to develop a mannerism or misspeak words that you as the instructor miss when you're concentrating. The other students, your mates, who are playing the role of new recruits, are savage in their observations during the debrief, or snigger and take the piss at a misspoken word or even your stance.

I remember a good mate of mine, Dave, a country boy with a Devon farmer's accent giving us a five-minute lecturette on his family farm. Short lecturettes are often used as a way to build confidence prior to conducting full 45-minute lessons. Dave was doing fine; very informative, clearly confident and cruising towards a good pass. After a slight pause to gain our attention, Dave proceeded to adopt a sturdy, upright position, slammed his hands onto his hips and in his deep farmer's accent bellowed "Chickens!"

Meant only as a transition into his next sub-topic, the combination of his stance, accent and the sincerity with which he bellowed "Chickens!" sparked spontaneous laughter and the total collapse of the class.

One thing the Army teaches you from day one is that a sense of humour is essential. It refines your skill in finding the funny side in absolutely anything. Many of you would have heard of a soldier's dark sense of humour, how we laugh at the most inappropriate topics, but I would ask you all to understand that the horrific things most soldiers will witness during their careers are such that if we didn't joke in adversity, find a way to lessen the traumatic scenes we've witnessed, many, many more would be taking their own lives.

Laughing helps you cope, it helps you compartmentalise the horror you just saw, the pain of leaving your family behind or seeing your mate torn apart. Hurling abuse at each other, teasing each other and practical jokes are all part of the toughening process required to do the job, and unless you have been there, you will never truly understand. understand. Our friends abused us to our faces but defended our backs from others.

The JNCO Cadre went very well for me, and I was awarded the position of Top Student and promoted to Lance Corporal on the last day of the Cadre by our CO, Lt Col Andrew Freemantle, who as a younger Lieutenant, had transferred to the Australian Special Air Service (SAS) and completed two tours of Vietnam before returning to the British Army.

Having come top of the course and attaining the rank of Lance Corporal within 15 months of joining, I felt sure my dad would be proud of me and, in his normal understated way, he was. To me though, all I saw was what my childhood issue had instilled in me– the feeling of not being good enough.

I moved from A Company to B Company on promotion - along with Sandy who had also done well and been promoted - and to a Company Commander whom I highly respect and learned a lot about leadership from, Major Nick Sim. Nick was an imposing man who looked like he would have been better employed smashing a Roman shield wall with an axe. He was a man who commanded respect.

Nick called me into his office not long after I had joined the company to tell me he was sending me to Junior Brecon in 5 weeks time. Junior Brecon is the British Army's battle course to qualify you up to Corporal. It is normal to remain a Lance Corporal for about three years before being considered, so as you can imagine, I was more than a little surprised. Again, I did very well on the course, gained the recommendation to go back as an instructor on the course and came back to the Regiment fully qualified for promotion.

Not long after this, we were told of our operational deployment to South Armagh in Northern Ireland, and I volunteered to join a covert unit that worked direct to "Group" the formation that contained all special operations units under its command, and so I had very little time to worry about when I would be promoted.

I had a pretty good relationship with the Commanding Officer. This came despite the fact that I had been the first soldier presented to him for punishment.

I'd been involved in a vehicle accident in Berlin and it led to CO's Orders, and the good chance I was going to end up in jail for a week or two. During this process, your Company Commander, in this case, Major Michael Reeve-Tucker; a good man who was to save me again later in my career at Court Martial, provides a character reference to help the CO decide on your punishment.

During this, as I was fairly new and a young Private soldier in rank, it included my TAVR service, and on mention of my previous unit, the CO looked up and directly at me for what felt like forever, before silently returning his gaze to the Military Police report on his desk. At the end of the proceedings, the CO asks if you accept his award, which normally involves a fine, jail, restriction of privileges, or wish for a Court Martial. I accepted his award, which consisted of him stepping from behind his desk and planting me, dropping me to the carpet without any further punishment. Pain was always a preferred option for soldiers as jail, or a fine, both hurt your wage packet.

I never missed the chance to remind my CO that he'd told me I was next to be promoted, and so when I was promoted to Corporal and took over my own covert 4-man team, I found myself passing the Col. Freemantle in the corridor in Bessbrook, our main base of operations. He congratulated me and asked if I would stop bothering him now!

I've never been too smart on when to keep my mouth shut and so, believing myself a comedian, I called out to the now continuing CO, "Do you have any Sgt vacancies, Sir?" Not sure I'll ever get over the trauma of the CO barrelling back down the corridor and delivering a few well-placed punches  into my collapsing frame as he laughed and called me an ungrateful bastard and told me that I was lucky he didn't punch my lights out. Ever the comedian.

"So that's a no, Sir?" was greeted with a shake of his head as he walked away. Lt Col Freemantle is a legend in our Regiment and transformed us into the fittest and most professional Regiment in the British Army.

Over the years, my continued success just never seemed enough to impress my dad, in my mind at least. It was only at his funeral that I was to discover just how proud of me he was. As my career continued to grow, I found myself as a Colour Sgt (CSGT) instructor at the British Army's Battle School at Brecon. I served as one of a highly specialised team of eight in the Sniper/SF Division during the late 1990s. It was a hard job, with many long days spent outside in the less than perfect Welsh weather, but one I loved. My time in this role was extended past my orders dates, which saw me serve three years in Brecon. During this time, I attended and passed all the sniper-related courses at the United States Marine Corps Sniper School, a unit I very much admire and was lucky enough to teach at their Sniper Schools on multiple occasions as a guest instructor. My USMC Identity Card is still a cherished possession.

The long days often meant that come Friday, all you wanted to do was grab a few beers in the Warrant Officers' and Sgts' Mess with your mates, and head home to sleep. My parents lived around four hours from the school by car, which seemed a long way to drive back then.

One week, I had told them I'd be down with their grandkids on Saturday morning. Come the morning, I just did not want to spend four hours in a car with weekend traffic, and so I decided we would go on a different weekend. To avoid the back and forth with my mum as to why I wasn't coming, I selfishly decided to just leave them hanging. Wrong, rude and cowardly in so many ways, but I just didn't want the hassle.

At around 1730 (5:30 p.m.) on Sunday, my house phone rang. I answered the phone and was surprised to hear my dad's voice. Dad never called anyone. if he answered it at all it was only to say, "hang on, I'll get your mother," and he was gone. So, the sound of my dad's voice immediately sent my heart into overdrive as I knew something was wrong, and if it was my dad calling it had to be Mum...

"Dad, is something wrong?"

My worst fears seemed to be coming true as he replied, "Actually, son, there is."

Bracing for the worst I listened as my dad said, "Son, if you say you're coming down, come down. I waited all weekend to see you."

There was only the slightest quiver in my dad's voice, but it was enough to reduce me to tears. Why? It was the first time in my life that I truly knew my dad loved me and that my actions had deeply hurt him. I told him how sorry I was, and that wild horses wouldn't stop me driving down the coming Friday. He told me that would make him happy, and we hung up. I went upstairs to our bedroom and cried.

That Wednesday morning, at 4 a.m., my mum called to tell me that Dad had a sudden heart attack, which took his life.

I never got to see him again. The last memory I have of Dad, my hero, was that I'd let him down and he died, disappointed in me. This was a memory that was to haunt me for several years to come.

My father's funeral was a fairly low-key affair, mostly family. I wore my dress uniform and medals in his honour as we dressed him in his Regimental Tie and Blazer. I was, therefore, pleasantly surprised to see 15 former Tigers, all dressed in their own Regimental Ties and Blazers, arrive. Some of these soldiers hadn't seen my dad in over 30 years and yet came from all over the country to show he was not forgotten.

They all came to me after, paying respects to Mum, and all, to a man, knew

Me and my Dad at the Laying up of our Colours. See

who I was and told me how much Dad talked about me to them on the phone and how proud of me he was. It was a bittersweet moment. I realised that, for all these years, I was wrong, and was devastated by the knowledge that my last act to my proud father was to let him down because I simply couldn't be bothered. When the Regimental buglers, who attended at my request, played the Last Post, I lost it.

The shame and guilt of my actions haunted me. Father's Day was a harrowing experience, reminding me that I didn't have one anymore and instigating a fight with the feelings of guilt I held over the way he passed. Each year, Father's Day brought to life these feelings, making me emotional– a weakness that the Army breeds out of you. You can't afford to show weakness in the Army.

———————————◆

I know now that emotion is not weakness, not in civilian life, but in the Army, emotional strength and resilience are a prerequisite of the job. They spend years training you to hide your emotions, to act in a cold, logical way. It's needed, a soldier cannot function any other way. A husband, though, a father, a civilian, they need those emotions. But the Army spends next to no time retraining your emotions when you leave. We are not taught to channel our feelings, how to talk about them or how to adjust to a world that is led by emotion. The result is that many, many soldiers fail to adjust, especially in today's ever-offended world, where everything from their sense of humour to their work ethic and attitude is deemed out of date and wrong– all adding to the pressure these men and women are already fighting inside.

———————————◆

It was only during an operational tour of Kosovo that I finally found peace with the death of my dad. I was by now a Sgt Major and, as Father's Day came around, I found myself struggling to remain focused, suppress my emotions and hold on enough to not cry. During the day, our Padre came down to our outstation to visit with the guys. I had seen many Padres in my career and had zero time for any of them– they represented a version of God I did not agree with.

Our current Padre, though, was something else. A former nightclub bouncer in his hometown of Liverpool, this Padre was anything but your archetypical man of God, in so much as he had tattoos and named his Pitbull Satan!

During his visit, he pulled me to one side and asked, "What's wrong, Sgt Major?"

It didn't matter how many times I brushed him off and told him nothing, he just kept looking at me, until I finally found myself tearing up and told him, "Let's go and grab a brew."

Being forward located in a Kosovan Police Station, we had use of their small café, and while it was a pleasant break from the portacabins we called home, it was also a test of your immune system– hygiene wasn't particularly high on the agenda.

The café was typically laid out, with small tables and chairs with the counter being the normal glass-fronted shelving displaying the options to go with your chi. The edges of the various sandwiches usually looked like Aladdin's slippers where they'd been in the heat of the day for hours and were curling up at the edges. It wasn't uncommon to see a mouse chowing down on sandwiches inside the cabinet.

As we sat chilling with our chi, I explained my issue to the Padre. At the end of my story, he explained my options.

One stood out in particular; "Write your dad a letter. Explain everything you just said to me and ask him to show you he isn't mad at you."

"How do I do that?"

"Come on Sgt Major, you're a resourceful man. You'll think of a way. Write the letter, and you can mail it with no return address. Or, you could tie it to a balloon and watch it float away or burn it and watch the smile go."

Once we finished our chi, I thanked him and headed back to my room, deep in thought.

───────────◆

Now, if you've learned anything about me so far, it should be that I'm highly logical and pragmatic, as are many service personnel both before and after me. Logic, order and emotional disconnection are all skills encouraged and actively taught in the Armed Forces. So, in my initial musings, I was sceptical of the advice that the Padre gave me. Don't get me wrong, I saw the value in it, but I initially viewed it as something that would help someone else, someone that wasn't me. But the truth is, no logical or pragmatic approach had worked before. Logic and pragmatism hadn't served me particularly well in dealing with emotional issues in the past.

This leads me to my advice; be willing to try new things when it comes to managing your mental wellbeing. The mind, however we try to train it, is not a logical place, where everything sits in order ready for us to sift through and access where needed. The brain's chemistry is extremely complex– it doesn't take much to create chemical imbalances that affect our mental state.

Writing things down, like letters to loved ones, is an incredibly effective way of getting negative thoughts that are swirling around our brains out, onto paper, in a place where we can visualise them, process them and come to terms with them. I believe, based on my experience, that this is an incredibly useful tool, particularly for vets and ex-service personnel, and even for those of us who think in predominantly logical ways, to come to terms with the thoughts we can't otherwise express. It is useful for the operators, those who think in straight lines, rationally, to make sense of that which we need to rationalise and create objectives and goals.

————————————◆

Later that night, I wrote to my dad. It took several attempts, was interrupted by tears, but I eventually had just one thing left to write. How could I ask my dad to show me if he was not mad at me?

I eventually settled on a very ambiguous challenge and wrote, "Dad, if you are not disappointed in me, find me, show me you know where I am." I don't think I even know what I meant by that, but it seemed enough. It was now two in the morning and most of the guys not on duty were crashed out in their pits. Out the back of our accommodation was a small fenced-in area where the guys could sit, chat or smoke, and there was only one way out there. I didn't want to be seen or asked why I was sat watching an envelope burn, and so I found an ashtray, my lighter and walked out into the dark. The good thing about our temporary home was that there was no creeping up on someone because the floors creaked too much, so, I was confident I wouldn't be caught unawares by one of my men.

Sat in the dark, I lit the envelope on one corner, placed it into the ashtray and watched the smoke drift up into the darkness.

I felt better. I truly did. A part of me, though, remained doubtful that feeling would last. About three days later, I was talking to my mum on a call home when she suddenly asked me, "Is the football stadium still there or was it destroyed in the bombing?"

To say the question took me by surprise would be an understatement.

"How did you know there was a football stadium in Pristina, Mum?"

"Oh, your dad loved that stadium! We watched two games there when it was still Yugoslavia and we went on holiday there, your dad loved the place!"

I had no idea my parents had ever been to Pristina, and I was left with no doubts that Dad had just shown me he knew where I was and that he was keeping an eye on me.

Suicide, Murder, and Setbacks

The following section contains further descriptions of emotional trauma, pain and suicide. Once again, I urge caution as you progress throughout this section. You may well encounter similarities with your own experiences or feel yourself becoming emotionally exposed by some of the experiences and events detailed.

You see, my own experiences with PTSI were not linked to any one event. Yes, certain events triggered it and made it worse, heightening its symptoms. But the roots of my PTSI, and that of so many others, developed over the course of a sequence of events and the emotional damage those events did– and how they went untreated.

As I mentioned at the very beginning of this book, PTSI is an injury. An event, a trauma, has damaged the mind of the victim, and just like with a physical injury, if it isn't treated correctly and early enough, the injury grows in severity. That injury is more likely to inflict permanent damage that the victim never fully heals from.

If, however, we treat the injury early enough, and in the correct way, we negate the effects of the injury. We may not treat it entirely, there may be a niggle that persists or a sensitivity, but we come far closer to full recovery, or at the very least, something that is manageable.

Often, we continue to receive treatment for the injury. If it is a physical injury, we may have regular physiotherapy. If it is mental, as in the case of PTSI, this may take the form of counselling or seeing a psychiatrist. When we see a physiotherapist, they often give us exercises to complete at home; stretches, weightlifting, yoga, among many others. We buy into these as recipients because you can physically feel the effects of them. Your strength grows and the effects of your injury diminish as you recover.

The same happens when we receive treatment for a mental condition. We are often given tasks to complete at home or in our own time. This may include writing letters, diaries, taking medication or attending various groups. The difference is that the results of this are not as immediately obvious as with a physical injury. The brain is a tumultuous place, our feelings are not always clear and the exercises open us up to feelings of vulnerability.

The difficulty with PTSI is that you often feel absolutely nothing. You feel as though you are in the right, so why does everybody else not feel as you do? At least, that's how it felt for me and for many of the other victims of PTSI that I have spoken to. Therefore, the treatment we are prescribed often feels wrong or daft, like it doesn't apply, like it won't work. This, for me, is why so many sufferers of PTSI end up succumbing to the Darkness.

What helped in my case was self-reflection and mindfulness. When we feel as though the prescribed treatment isn't relevant to us because we are not the problem, often the solution is self-reflection, through meditation or just thinking about the successes and failures of the day. Critical appraisal of our performance throughout the day, for the operators out there, helps us to identify where perhaps we made the mistakes, where we didn't seek treatment fast enough or recognise the symptoms of our conditions. Through this, we allow ourselves to grow, actively seeking to correct the errors of our ways and not repeat the same mistakes we made before.

In each of the examples that follow, an injury was dealt to my psyche, to my mind, and in each of them, the issue was buried, treatment not sought. With each subsequent trauma, the symptoms grew and developed, damaging me further to the point where recovery became a more distant goal. As you read through, you may begin to identify some of the instances in your life that contribute to your own trauma, or that of your loved ones. I hope that this broadens the scope of your awareness, allowing you to probe deeper within your own feelings, and those of the people you love.

————————◆

Shane

Diane's suicide was not the first I had witnessed at close range.

Back in the late 80s, I was part of a highly specialised covert surveillance unit. Our job was to put terrorists under 24-hour surveillance at extremely close ranges– sometimes even from inside their own homes. To be a member of this unit, the guys had to pass a selection course that was intensely physically demanding, forcing teams to endure extremes of weather (the cold, the hot, the dry, the wet), often for weeks at a time whilst achieving operational success and remaining concealed. The course was, out of necessity, extremely demanding.

The unit fell under command of the Group, a covert element of British Special Operations and so only accepted the very best a Battalion had to offer. The pre-deployment training was long and incorporated, on average, 19-hour days. These days often blurred into one– exhaustion and sleep deprivation were the norm, to the point where it became difficult to differentiate one day from the next. We mainly worked at night, identifying a position from which to gather evidence, occupying that position and camouflaging ourselves. We then settled into a routine of surveillance.

Our training was focused on observation, camouflage, concealment and evidence-gathering. On top of this, there was an intense focus on photography and repetitive drills, refining our close-quarter combat skills.

One day in particular will remain with me, and with the other members of the team, for the rest of our lives.

The teams had just finished a long day on the range performing ambush after ambush with live-firing drills and were all looking forward to a shower and a few beers. As we arrived back at camp and began making our way into our building, we were stopped by the Regimental Police and told we couldn't go into our room as there was an incident underway. This incident involved a guy I knew well, Shane, who was currently pending a Court Martial for giving his mates in the Battalion unauthorised travel passes so they could get home for free on weekends on public transport.

I had first met Shane while in Basic Training in Whittington Barracks, just outside the city of Lichfield. Shane and I were in different platoons but were both transitioning to the same unit and so, we spent many nights chatting. Like most military bases, once a week a "disco" was held on base and a steady stream of young women looking for fun, and a possible way out of their hometown, would arrive by bus or car for what the guys called "The Dogs Ball"; a less than flattering term, gained in part by the girls who dated guys throughout their Basic Training and then moved onto another as soon as he deployed to his unit.

As you can imagine, these particular girls were well known to the recruits and were not highly regarded outside of carnal lust. Shane fell head over heels for one of these girls, married her, and brought her to the Battalion where several of her previous "boyfriends" still remembered her. In true fashion, they took the piss out of him relentlessly.

Shane was under open arrest, which meant he could move freely around the base, but wasn't allowed off base and had to report to the Guard Room and Regimental Police at certain times of the day. At his visit to the Guard Room at 1200 hours, he saw an opportunity to walk out with a rifle and took it. Nobody knows why he chose our room to barricade himself in, but he had, and nobody knows why he waited until a certain time of the day to act.

On arrival at our building, we could see the Commanding Officer, Tim, leaning through a ground floor window directly under the external stairs that led to the upper floor rooms. The Regimental Sgt Major, Vic, and a few of the Regimental Police were also close to the situation, keeping a safe, yet fairly close, distance. I stepped out of my vehicle and beckoned one of them over, a fella called Andy and asked him what the score was.

Andy told me that Shane had taken a loaded rifle from the Guard Room and barricaded himself in the room. He had locked the door and barricaded it with furniture and put a locker in front of the window, which was the only other way in the room. Following this, he had perched himself on the corner bed, leaning against the wall with the rifle in his lap.

When it was noticed that the rifle was missing from the rack, a search was made for Shane. He was the only person to have entered the Guard Room other than the guys on guard, and they found him in our room. He was refusing to come out, threatening to shoot anyone who tried to get in. He had given no indication of his intent, but suicide was clearly an option. Somebody told the RSM that I knew Shane, so he called me over and asked if I would talk to him, and I found myself replacing the CO at the window.

I had a limited view due to the moved locker, but I could see Shane, and he could see me. He broke into a wide smile, and he greeted me with an enthusiastic "Hey, Spice!" to which I asked him what the fuck he was doing.

"Could you not have done this in your own fucking room, you selfish twat!" Humour is always the first choice for Brits, and I saw his smile grow wider still.

"You special fuckers get all the best stuff, so I thought I might as well enjoy it for a while," He chipped back at me, laughing.

"Yeah, that worked out well didn't it mate? We get the same shite you do; now can you stop fucking about so we can have a fucking shower!" I tried to keep it casual, hoping that my casual attitude would transfer across to him. It didn't.

"I can't mate, I'm done," the smile on his face dropped, settling into a look of defeat and resignation.

He told me he'd had enough; he was fed up and wanted to see what was on the other side.

"Shane... mate, stop for a second and think. If you're properly serious about this, why now? Why have you waited for this long? You've been in here since midday mate! Doesn't that tell you something? That you're not sure, you're not done. You need to stop and think about everything mate." He looked up at me, a look of uncertainty etched across his face. I wondered if he was worried about

97

the consequences of his actions, if he was stalling because he was worried about any potential punishment.

"Mate, the boys outside have all offered you help, even fucking Tim! They know that this is you crying out for help, mate. We all know that this is no crime, so they ain't gonna beast you for it. Why don't you put the rifle down, come out and let us help you?" I'd dropped humour at this point, opting for empathy and understanding.

The RSM was outside with the Regimental Police Staff brain-storming ways in which they could force entry without giving Shane the time to shoot himself or them. A suggestion was made to sledgehammer the door open and, as the first person rushed the door through the door, who in this scenario would be the RSM, they would chuck a cricket ball at him to induce an instinctive reaction to buy the required time to reach him. Thankfully, that idea was abandoned when it was pointed out how heavy those old doors were and that a single sledgehammer blow wouldn't be enough for immediate entry.

Whenever a watch alarm goes off, everyone instinctively looks to check it wasn't theirs. The alcove under the stairwell where we were standing amplified the sound of the alarm that had suddenly started, and after checking my watch I looked up to see the same confused look on everyone's faces as each of us confirmed it wasn't theirs. We quickly looked around and spotted a watch on the floor, right under the bottom step. Earlier in the stand-off, the CO had talked Shane out of his watch, and he had thrown it out the open window. The CO and I both realised at the same time whose watch it was and spun to put our heads through the window.

I can honestly say that I have never seen a calmer man. Shane casually rested the rifle butt on his thigh, smiled at me and put the barrel in his mouth. He held my gaze as he pulled the trigger and the CO reeled back as the gun fired. The RSM, Vic, saw me shoving the locker out of the way to get into the room through the window and pushed with me until it toppled.

I reached Shane first, closely followed by Vic. Shane was still leaning in the corner on the bed and I grabbed his foot and pulled him flat so we could work on him. Being on a bed meant that every time we tried to compress his chest, the mattress absorbed it, so we lifted him off the bed and onto the floor. Vic unloaded the rifle, threw it on the bed opposite and joined me in trying to resuscitate Shane.

Included in the kit we took on our exercises was a plastic airway. I'd put mine in my pocket when I was told was what happening and had now fitted it into Shane's mouth, hoping it would somehow reach past the wound and we could get some air into him. It didn't, and instead it just acted as a tap. I was also vaguely aware of a loud thumping, but it was not until the Unit Doctor arrived next to us that I realised it was them battering their way in through the door with a sledgehammer.

"Forget it," he told us, "He's gone."

It was pretty obvious by his wounds Shane wasn't going to recover, but you just can't stop or give up, you have to try, and we kept going until the MO pulled me back and said, "It's over, there's nothing we can do."

After being told we could give our witness statements later, Vic and I agreed to meet in the Warrant Officer's and Sgt's Mess. Vic's idea; he was clear in his insistence that we both needed a drink. We both washed up, changed out of our blood-stained uniforms and met in the bar. We sat together in the Mess in a heavy silence and after three whiskeys each, Vic said, "Ok then, back to work," and we both got to our feet and left.

The Army way of compartmentalising everything kicked in; we both manned up and went back about our business with the images of what we'd seen now burned into our memories.

As it turned out, Shane had left a letter addressed to the CO and in it, he explained, as he had said to me, that he had just had enough and wanted to see if he would be happier on the other side. He never explained why he chose 3 p.m. to take his life, but, unknown to any of us, he had set his alarm and the echo and amplification caused by the stairwell was enough for him to hear it from the room.

In his letter, he told the CO that he loved the Army, loved the Battalion and that he was sorry if he embarrassed the Battalion, but he was done. He asked to be buried as a soldier, which in the case of suicide is not permitted, but the CO made it happen anyway and Shane was taken to Tidworth Military Cemetery on a gun carriage and buried with full military honours. To this day, the lads clean and put a poppy on his grave every Remembrance Day.

———————◆

Sutty

I have always taken the welfare of the men I lead incredibly seriously, and the lads knew my integrity was very important to me, so my open-door policy was well known if they had issues. This policy is important to me to this day, especially in my current work. It is essential that leaders are open and attentive to the needs of the team, and they remove all of the barriers needed and appropriate to facilitate open communication.

When units deploy, it is not uncommon for small groups of soldiers to be moved to a safe area to enable them to engage in some form of sport. This may include canoeing, rock climbing or parachuting, with the ultimate goal of helping relieve stress and giving them a much-needed break. Our deployment to Northern Ireland was no different.

Pte. Sutton, widely known as Sutty, was a 19-year-old soldier in my platoon, and one of the most motivated soldiers I had commanded. He was always first to volunteer for extra patrols, duty or just about anything related to soldiering. On a cool mid-Friday afternoon, Sutty walked to my office door, slammed his foot to the floor and assumed the position of attention.

"What have you done now Sutton?" was my initial response, to which he smiled and asked if he could have a word. He explained to me in the ensuing conversation that he had been signed up for a weekend adventure training event. I couldn't see the issue, and my initial, internal response, which perhaps marred the rest of the conversation, was dismissive. Lucky fucker, why did I need to know, and what could he possibly have to complain about? He carried on, explaining to me that it was a rock-climbing event, and he didn't want to go.

He further explained that he'd been approached by another soldier who wanted to go in his place, and when he approached our Sgt Major, he had been told to stop whining and that he was going, like it or not. He asked if I would be willing to approach the Sgt Major on his behalf and get him out of it?

Initially, I'd adopted the same view as the Sgt Major. After all, he'd potentially learn a new skill, bond with some of the lads and blow off some steam. It was precisely that reasoning, though, that his request threw me off guard. He was a hard worker, and so naturally would jump at the chance for some fun and a chance to try something different. I reasoned that there was a reason he wasn't telling me about, and his body language, fidgety hands and willingness to ask this favour of me told me all I needed to know. He was anxious, perhaps scared, and a day of what was supposed to be light-hearted fun would not be the right time to test his limits and potentially embarrass him in front of the lads.

Now, at the time, I had a good relationship with the Sgt Major, even though friends had warned me he should work in a circus with his ability to throw knives and backstab, but I'd given him the benefit of the doubt. I was to regret that later in my career when his backstabbing led to my Court Marshal.

I was somewhat taken aback when I approached the Sgt Major on Sutty's behalf, and he dismissed me out of hand. He told me he was done with the subject, and he wasn't changing any paperwork late on a Friday afternoon.

I returned to my office and with my sincerest apologies, gave Sutty the bad news that he was going. He shrugged, thanked me for trying and trudged off. I never really thought about it over the weekend; I was on duty, so my weekend was pretty much business as usual.

Monday morning soon came along, and as I was walking to my office, another of my young soldiers stopped me and, with a look of concern on his face, asked, "Did you hear about Sutty, Sir?"

"No, what has he done now?" I asked, wondering how he'd managed to embarrass or make a fool of himself. Along with Sutty's keenness came an element of rebellion, something that reminded me of myself, and it would not be the first time I'd have been needed to sort out a drunken fight, he'd been late back to camp or he'd been in the middle of a missed transport issue. I wasn't ready for the answer.

"Uh... He's dead, Sir."

Sutty, to his eternal credit, had indeed gone on the rock-climbing trip; typical of his normal can-do attitude and willingness to not disappoint. While climbing, he had lost his footing, slipped, and fallen 30 feet, smashing the back of his head onto a lower ledge.

The JNCO in charge had climbed as fast as he could to reach him, and he found Sutty alive but suffering serious head injuries. Tragically, Sutty passed before they could get help to him.

I was immediately overcome with guilt. Why hadn't I argued harder on his behalf? Why had I allowed him to be pushed into something he didn't want to do? I was to argue this point loudly with the Sgt Major some 15 minutes later, before being threatened with close arrest if I didn't shut up and remember my place. It didn't matter; it was too late; nothing was bringing him back. Sutty is buried in the same cemetery as Shane, and the lads visit him often.

Two Tigers

I remember asking my dad, not long after I had joined the Army, what was his most vivid memory– the hardest thing he did in the Army? I was somewhat surprised and, at the time, a little disappointed, in his answer. I had expected something like a battle course, jungle warfare or a long ruck march or something of that nature, and so when he said, "bury two of our men," I was taken by surprise.

My dad had been involved in the burial of soldiers who lost their lives fighting drug dealers in Jamaica in the late '50s and I still have the photos of the funerals, so I knew what event he was talking about. But it wasn't until I was in my last few weeks with the British Army that I finally understood.

During my resettlement period - the time the Army tries to find you a new job  by sending you to a plumber or electrician's class, but completely ignores your mental welfare - I was left in the UK while my unit deployed to Iraq. One afternoon, I was called to the Rear Party Commander's office.

"Sgt Major, we've lost one," he told me, solemnly.

"Who? Do I know him?" I always hated these conversations.

"Young Chris Rayment."

I did know him; I knew him very well. He had been in my Company and deployed to Kosovo with us. It was a blow to think that Chris, who was affectionately known as Ray and a proper full of life sort of bloke; very similar to Sutty in attitude, was gone. It wasn't long before we knew there was a second, another young Tiger called Lee O'Callaghan, who was killed in an operation to rescue some other soldiers who'd got themselves into trouble, cornered and pinned down inside a house, Lee was a part of the rescue team that went in, and while they got all the guys out safely, Lee was hit in the neck and died from his injuries.

I don't think anything can prepare you for the image that is presented as you slow march up the tail ramp of a C17; a cavernous aircraft able to carry 100 soldiers, with a lone coffin sat in the middle of the aircraft, draped in the Union Jack of the United Kingdom. An image so small, and yet an image that blurs out the rest of the aircraft, more powerful and profound that a plane full of soldiers

Once we were aboard it occurred to me that if that image had such a profound effect on me mentally, it was likely to have done the same to my team.

"OK lads, take a couple of minutes to compose yourself. If you want to say goodbye personally, now's the time, he was family."

Several of the guys knelt, placed their hands on the coffin and bowed their heads, some stood silent in prayer. Each of the lads, some of them normally study and unmoving, was impacted and moved by both the image of that lone coffin and the solemn atmosphere inside that aircraft.

My burial party consisted of soldiers wounded in combat in Iraq and home convalescing, and brand-new soldiers straight from training, whose first job in the Army was to bury two of their new family.

Welcome to the Army.

I called them back to order and reminded them that the family was standing right next to the Hearse, and for their sakes, we had to do as dignified a job as was humanly possible. Soldiers are always briefed not to cry when being a part of the funeral party, and that in itself is a very hard ask as you pass a grieving mother watching her son come home under a flag. You feel as if you let her down by losing him.

I have never been a drill soldier; marching up and down just never did it for me. I had managed to avoid all drill parades since we changed from the SLR rifle to the SA80 in 1988 and it was now 2004, no mean feat! I was a field soldier through and through.

One of the best compliments I ever received was from the comments your Commanding Officer writes on your annual report when my CO wrote:

"Sgt Spicer is a warrior and a field soldier; he would not have been out of place in a Roman Legion." So, you can understand why this current task had me questioning my ability to give the fallen men and their families the funerals they deserved. The thought troubled me greatly and I made a decision.

I wrote a letter to the London District RSM, the senior Sgt Major in the Army, to explain my mindset and to request, for the sake of the lads we had lost, that a better-suited Sgt Major take over the managing of the funerals. I was taken a little by surprise when he called me and, for over 40 minutes, he told me how many have the same fears, that he was there to help and that I could do this. So I faced my fear and I trained in my room every night in the build-up to the funeral until the early hours of the morning, determined to do the best I could.

Both of the lads were Londoners, born and raised in the Nation's capital, so both funerals would be in London with the associated traffic and congestion, which any Londoner, or indeed any visitor to London knows well.

I have to praise the motorcycle officers of the Metropolitan Police, who rode ahead of us stopping traffic, so we never had to stop at lights during both the rehearsals and the actual funerals. They were amazing.

In the Army, everything is practised and refined until it is instinctive and so, the day before each funeral, we carried out a full-dress rehearsal, in London, on our actual route and timings, but with a weighted coffin. We did this for both funerals.

For Lee's funeral it had been requested, and granted, that we drive past his favourite football stadium, The Den, home of Millwall Football Club, on our way to the cemetery. Lee had been an avid Millwall fan his whole life, and his parents wanted to take him to the stadium one last time.

During the rehearsal, we reached the gates of the stadium, and, as planned, the men took up station on either side of the vehicle and we began the slow march past the main doors of the stadium. There was a building site opposite us, and as we marched through, I noticed that all the builders working on the site had stopped working and removed their hard hats in respect.

This show of respect for our fallen brother, who was not currently there with us, moved me almost to tears. With a tear escaping my eye, I walked across the site and informed the site foreman that it was a rehearsal, and while we appreciated their gesture, this was not his actual funeral. He thanked me for letting them know and asked when the actual funeral was, and I told him it would be the following day. I reassured him that as it was a Saturday, it would not impact their work.

The following day, as we approached the stadium, the scene that greeted us is one that I will never forget, and one that will remain with me for the rest of my life.

As the convoy turned into the stadium car park, stood in front of us were the owners and players of Millwall F.C., lined up in silent tribute to one of their fans who had given his life to freedom. On the opposite side were the site foreman and his staff, on their day off, all waiting to pay their respects to a fallen soldier, a son of London.

As we slow marched past, it was impossible to contain our emotions. We defied orders, allowing the tears to roll down our faces as each in turn bowed their heads. Brits have long-held respect for their soldiers, and it was overwhelmingly moving to see it up close.

The same happened at Ray's funeral. The church was located right next to a large shopping area, and when we arrived, the streets were already lined with people who had left their jobs in the neighbouring stores or stopped their shopping to stand in silence as we brought their fallen son home to London.

London is a city that has had its fair share of war, and it was plain to see they had not forgotten.

These funerals, and the events that surrounded them, represented a particularly emotional period for me, and for the first time, I truly understood Dad's comments all those years before. There are few things more emotionally challenging than burying a fellow soldier; a man or woman who has given their all for their country and their mates, given up all their tomorrows in defence of freedom.

Looking back on pictures of the day still, to this day, brings to life all of those emotions, and I have no doubt that it left a similar mark on the other guys as well. In true Army fashion, though, we compartmentalised it and soldiered on, until the day it comes back to visit, as it always does.

Limavady

S oldiers are often misjudged or misunderstood because of politics or opinion, and in Northern Ireland, it was no different. The Catholic communities saw us as the enemy in general. The IRA had a very efficient propaganda machine and the deep-seated religious beliefs of many meant that soldiers were automatically viewed as cold, killing machines.

One weekend, I was driving down a main road, off duty, towards a small town called Limavady. The road was fairly typical of Ireland, with rolling hills and blind turns and so I wasn't taken entirely by surprise as I rounded a bend to see a car accident a few hundred metres in front.

Our covert unit training trains us to have a heightened sense of caution on blind bends, as it wasn't uncommon to find an illegal IRA vehicle checkpoint appear suddenly on the other side. These illegal checkpoints operated in a similar way to the highwaymen of old, where they "invited" people to "donate to the cause" in a poorly disguised attempt at robbery. As a result, I was already prepared to slow down or speed up as I approached the blind bend.

For an off-duty soldier on his own, it isn't safe to stop and converse with strangers miles from anywhere, but the accident looked bad and there were obvious signs of panic. Reluctantly and cautiously, I pulled up in front of the lead vehicle to allow me a clear escape route, checked my rear-view mirror again, and decided to see if I could help.

A quick assessment of the scene made it clear that the accident was caused by a speeding car cutting the corner and clipping the oncoming car, spinning it into a dry-stone wall. It soon became apparent that the major injury was in that car. As I approached, I could see several of the queuing cars had rosary beads hanging from their rear-view mirrors; a clear indication that most of them were catholic. I decided that I had best be on my guard.

Among the onlookers and bystanders still in their cars were distressed parents leaning into the back seat to settle their kids and several people standing around doing nothing. Taking charge, I directed some to move to the rear of the accident and slow any oncoming traffic down to avoid any additional collisions, and told two others to call for an ambulance; you can't afford to rely on one individual where life is concerned. and the dispatch would work out that it's the same incident and only send what was needed.

In most cases, a strong voice and confident delivery are enough to spark most people into action. After moving people out of my way, I climbed into the totalled car and directed the male - the driver - to make sure that the engine was off, the handbrake was on and to check the car for any damage that could cause a fire. One of the onlookers shouted that there was fuel leaking onto the ground, but there seemed no immediate risk of fire.

On the back seat was a young girl, around 15, who had been sat leaning on the offside rear door with her legs stretched across the back-seat foot area and resting on the prop shaft tunnel. At the moment of impact, the force had caused the car to crumple, the seats to move, and had trapped her leg for long enough to break it. She was in extreme pain and her leg was bent at an abnormal angle in the gap that was left.

"Okay, sweetheart, here's what I'm going to do. I need to check your leg to see if you have any other injuries. Don't worry, I'm not gonna hurt you. I just need you to lie still. Can you do that for me?" She nodded through tears and gritted teeth.

It was quickly apparent that she had broken her femur; the thigh bone, and the largest bone in the body. An injury that is already painful enough, the force of a breaking femur can easily sever the main artery that runs down the leg, past the bone, and so I had to look for signs of internal bleeding. As the bone hadn't pierced the skin, any internal bleeding would show as swelling and bruising, but with the femoral artery being a main artery, the risk of a quick death from blood loss was dangerously high.

I was fairly confident the break hadn't severed the artery considering the time she had already been sat there– but it pays to check. After a quick check, there were no signs of swelling past what I would have expected and no immediate bruising.

She was clearly in intense pain and growing increasingly distressed, so I wanted to ease her pain and settle her nerves as much as I could.

"Ok, it doesn't look like there's any extra damage, so here's what I want to do," I began to explain, "I want to move your bad leg. I know this is going to hurt, but I want to support it using your good leg, which will help ease the pain and make it less likely to get any worse. Is that ok?"

Understandably, she looked afraid and reluctant, so I explained to her, "I know it's scary, but either me or the paramedics when they get here will have to do it to get you out of the car with as little pain as possible."

A bond of trust was already building between us. She looked me in the eye, squared her jaw, and said, "Ok," nodding frantically.

"I'm not gonna lie to you, this will hurt, but you're in charge here. If you need me to stop, tell me and I'll stop straight away." I shouted for some bandages, which one of the onlookers passed to her dad - the driver - who in turn passed them to me. I gently cupped her leg above and below the break, had her dad cup her ankle, and we slowly lifted her broken leg onto the back seat in line with her other leg.

She was astonishingly brave and never made a sound past a stifled moan, and with her leg now over the pre-laid supports, her father and I both removed our belts and I grabbed a fleece jacket that was on the back seat. I gently placed the jacket between her legs as padding and used the bandages and belts to hold her legs in place.

As we did this, the paramedics arrived and I stepped back, briefed the paramedic on the injuries I'd found, what treatment I'd given her and moved to leave when she asked me to go with her in the ambulance. For my own security, that was something I couldn't do, so I apologised to her, told her she was in good hands, and I went to leave.

Her father stopped me and thanked me before asking for my name and contact number. When I said I couldn't do that, the penny dropped, and I saw in his eyes that he had just realised I was a British soldier. I think this was the first time, removed from the adrenaline of helping his daughter, that he noticed my Southern English accent.

I said to him, "Please remember, we are not your enemy," shook his hand, and drove on my way. I never did find out what happened next, past my boss calling for me on Monday morning and asking if I had attended a vehicle accident on Saturday on the Limavady Road. He told me a man had called the base wishing to thank the soldier who helped his daughter, and the description and car sounded like me? I said it wasn't and left it at that.

Soldiers are often misunderstood. We're not cold-hearted killers. We're not inherently stupid or violent as most want to believe. We didn't join the army out of a desire to kill and maim; we joined out of a sense of belief in our respective countries' ways of life; the freedom to complain or disagree, and we are willing to risk our lives to protect them if called upon.

Now, does every soldier hope to be in combat at some stage? Of course we do, but it has nothing to do with wanting to kill another human being. It has everything to do with the individual wondering if he will have the courage to hold the line, not let his mates down and fight through fear. It's about self-belief and self-awareness; that the words you say about protecting those who cannot protect themselves are true, and that you do have the courage to give your all if required.

I grew up in the era of football hooliganism, and so every weekend as a Portsmouth supporter, I would go toe-to-toe with lads from another town, so I knew I would stand in a fistfight. But would I stand when bombs and bullets were in play? It's about knowing, it's about the belief in something bigger than yourself and a little curiosity; after all, if you saw how little soldiers get paid, you'd know for sure it isn't about the money!

———————◆

So, why did I choose to include that story at the end, about the girl on the road to Limavady and her horribly broken leg? Why did I choose to include a story that was not one with a negative outcome, linked to sorrow, betrayal, death and suicide?

The truth is, it's so overwhelmingly easy to focus on the negative. I could have selected one of the dozens of other stories I have where the outcome was not so positive. Well… I did it for a couple of reasons.

First, it is good to remind ourselves of some of the good we have achieved, when in our minds, we often view those challenging times with a degree of loathing and fear, a fear that it will take us back towards the Darkness. But to ignore those periods of our lives is to acknowledge that they ever happened when they absolutely and unequivocally did. I think it is important to have some memories of the good we have done during our time in service, after all, isn't that why we joined? Isn't that why we give years of our lives to our chosen profession or our life choices. To the military, or the police, or healthcare, the fire service, or even to having children, husbands or wives that we may one day lose or have lost.

We shouldn't shut out those periods of our lives for the fear of relapse and pain. We should take heart from the positive and remember the good that came from our decisions to take part in those stages of our lives. You've hopefully noticed that, in my recounting of Di's passing, I interspersed it with positive memories, ones that I can draw on even in my retelling of that event that took me to the darkest of places. You have this power too! Take the good with the bad, don't shut off years of your life.

Secondly, I did it because, in all that we do, somebody will view us as a bad guy. In the military, you have a literal enemy, so you are naturally hated by the opposition, but you are also impacted by people's perceptions of you as a soldier. But this is true of so many professions; the police, politics, healthcare… you name the job, the walk of life, and someone has pre-conceived negative perceptions of you.

If you know anything about The Troubles in Northern Ireland, then you know that it was an extremely hostile environment for an Englishman in Northern Ireland, and this conflict spilled onto the British mainland with many terrorist attacks happening in regular suburban streets. This event formed a bond between myself and someone that would naturally consider me as their enemy. When in the depths of PTSI, it is easy for us to see those outside of our suffering as the "the enemy." After all, to us, they don't understand our pain. They've lived a sheltered life; how could they possibly relate?

Don't hate them. The most remarkable bonds can be formed in adversity. There's a popular phrase in the UK: "Don't bite the hand that feeds." It means, quite simply, don't shun or turn on those that are willing to help. We don't need them to see things from our point of view, but we do need them to understand why we may act the way we do. Communicate, receive communication, and do your best to use your network of friends and allies to help you through the Darkness when it rears its ugly head. In the same vein, *you are not the bad guy.* You, or your loved one, or your friend, is carrying an injury. When we, or our friends, are injured, we both offer and accept support. An injury of the mind should be no different.

Betrayal and Karma:
God's Will Be Done

As I explained in the opening of this book, my life had all but collapsed around me following the death of Diane and had taken me to the darkest of places. Everyone told me about the stages of grief, and for years I told people I never went through an angry phase. On reflection though, I spent a long time in an angry phase. It wasn't apparent to me. PTSI doesn't *feel* like anything. It makes you feel like the most reasoning individual in the room, when in fact you're far from that.

You feel that everyone else is wrong and you question why they can't see that you are right about how you feel, or why you feel that way. This is invariably a consequence of the hurt, pain and anger that has consumed your insides and invaded your consciousness.

Looking back, I was a very angry man and one who had zero intentions of living. I spent money without concern, I didn't care what anyone thought of me, and I was furiously jealous at any couple who were in love or happy; to the point of actually flirting or making inappropriate comments to friends' wives. These actions I sincerely apologise for and ask, for anyone affected, please research PTSI and learn its symptoms and dangers. At times, the victim of PTSI truly can't help themself. I can remember multiple occasions, creating or exacerbating awkward social situations, propagating and instigating conflict, saying to myself inside, "don't say, don't say it," and then hearing myself say that which I was willing myself to not say.

After losing Diane, it was about five years before I seriously wanted to share my life with someone else and love again. I'd had one-night stands; brief sex-based relationships before, but it was all fake, unreal, and I remember how bad I felt the first time I had sex after Diane passed; like I had cheated on her. As I came out of the depths of grief, I had developed a mentality of "use and leave" as far as women were concerned and I was adamant I would never love or allow myself to be hurt like that again.

The fact is, life doesn't always work the way you want, and over the years I have found that the phrase "God's Will Be Done" wasn't conceived without cause. The reason behind certain events, pain and unexpected direction changes is often that you're on the wrong path, with the wrong person, or need a push to where life wants you.

While I have struggled with trauma, job loss and other seemingly bad events, I have eventually come to realise that the results, often years later, suddenly allow you to see how they actually worked in your favour. When I talk to people about my belief that every tragedy conceals a gift, I am often scoffed at, or people tell me I'm an idiot. They ask me, "What was the gift in Diane's suicide?" In response, I point out two things that, in my eyes, were gifts.

Firstly, it made me a better man. The loss of my wife and the circumstances behind it forced me to re-evaluate who I was, how I acted and allowed me to grow as a human being. Secondly, for at least four years, I bemoaned the 12 minutes it took the paramedics to arrive. I convinced myself and outwardly complained that she may have lived if they had got there quicker. What could have taken them so long?

In reality, the damage Di had done to herself was so severe, nothing would have saved her. Then, one day, I can't remember exactly when, while I was moaning about it again I heard a voice in my mind tell me, "It was a gift."

That was it, just those words. Nothing else, and it was so clear it stopped me talking. Over the next few days, I pondered over those words, asking myself over and over; how could that be a gift? What am I missing here?

Sometimes in my life, quite a lot, to be honest, my mind's eye shows me a scene. At least, that's how it feels. I search my head for the answer to the "gift," and when I find it, it's as if the stage curtain rises and I just know. The smoke clears, the grass parts, and there it is, a warmness that feels like somebody is holding me. I remember when the realisation, the moment of awakening, came to me. I felt that warmth and a voice that made more sense than any I'd heard since Di's death.

"Who gets 12 minutes to say all the things they should have already said?"

At that moment I knew, God, Life, The Universe, whatever you choose to call it, had given me 12 minutes to say goodbye. They already knew she wouldn't make it. They knew this was my last chance to talk with her and for me, a gift to ease my pain at our parting, I was given 12 long minutes to talk to my wife and tell her how much I loved her. It's only when I look back, with this in mind, that I remember just how much I said to Diane in those 12 minutes. How I'd spilled into her every bit of love I had.

The second biggest stumbling block for me that also turned out to be a gift was solved by the words of Betty, Diane's mum. I struggled in my attempts to understand why Di would do this knowing I would be the one to find her, why would she hurt me in this way.

While asking that question, probably for the 100th time, Betty looked up and calmly said, "It had to be you. She knew you so well and she loved you so much, she knew it had to be you."

I didn't understand, and Betty continued, "She knew you had to be the one to find her, you had to see for yourself there was no saving her, or you would have torn yourself apart believing that if you had only been there, you could have saved her. She knew you had to try and fail if you were to have any chance of surviving this. She knew you."

That was a profound moment for me. Betty was right. I would have blamed myself for not being there, and while her actual death was a mistake, she had put the gun to her head probably multiple times in the weeks prior, and knew I had to be the one.

As time passed, I started to come out of my mind and look at the reality that maybe I could be happy again. Most people know I'm not happy being single. Some have accused me of having co-dependency issues. In truth, I have always been the same insomuch as I want someone in my life who loves me as much as I love them; a partner in crime, a soulmate. After all, what's the point of success in life if you have nobody to share it with, nobody to be excited about coming home to or waiting for you at the airport. That eventually led me to the realisation that I wanted somebody to love. Against all odds, I found myself craving a partner.

On the advice of a friend, I joined internet dating sites and learned all about swiping right or left, etc., and all the new-fangled ways people are supposed to meet. Now, I do have to say, that if all you want is sex, these sites are a gold mine! I went on maybe four dates, well, five if you count the one where I looked through the bar window and realised the picture was taken a decade ago and about-turned for my truck!

All of them were women whose profiles lectured on how annoying it was when men just wanted sex on the first date, only to offer sex on the first night. One I will never forget, a woman who offered me oral sex after telling me she was worried because she couldn't get a firefighter hard the night before on her last date, so she wanted to prove it was him and not her...errr...not for me, ta!

One night, I saw the profile of an attractive woman who had two teenage daughters and was a teacher. I remember thinking I was probably not her type.

The next day, I received a message from the app saying she had made me one of her favourites, so, not wanting to miss a chance, I messaged her, and she explained to me that she never knew it would tell me she did that and that she had done it so she could go back and look at my pictures later. Long story short, we met, clicked and ended up married about two years later.

Being a romantic at heart, I decided to suggest we get married in the UK, specifically in my hometown of Portsmouth. I then set about finding a castle to rent for the day so I could marry my wife in a castle in England. It just so happened that one of the castles in my hometown, Southsea Castle, was about to be opened to the public for events and weddings, and after a few phone calls and a trip home to speak with the office which controls their bookings, I secured the castle and a place in its history by being the first people allowed to marry in that castle outside the Royal Family! Result!

The wedding just happened to be on the 70th anniversary of D-Day, which meant that on the day, freefall parachute display teams, warships anchored off the coast and a booming firework display would all now, by default, be a part of our wedding.

The day itself went well... if you ignore the bride being almost two hours late... and with a castle all to ourselves until midnight, it was all very Cinderella. We partied the evening away without incident, which, considering the wedding party was made up of my mafia family and drunken soldiers, was in itself a miracle. I felt for sure that at least one of them would fall off the ramparts before the evening was over– a properly soldierly way to go!

At midnight, still in full party mood, we all walked across Southsea Common, a large, open grass area, to Palmerston Road where there were nightclubs, and joined the back of the line to get in.

Now, with so many of us in suits, fancily dressed and a bride in a full wedding dress, it wasn't long before the club bouncers came over to ask if it was a real wedding or a fancy-dress night out. When they learned it was real, they took our whole party to the front and gave us free entry.

The rest of the evening, and now early morning, was spent drinking, dancing on tables and me on the receiving end of the drunken lectures from many random women, telling me to be good and take care of my wife, and that if I hurt her, they would find me! If only they knew, maybe they could have come to rescue me instead!

Guess It Wasn't To Be...

She wasn't a bad person, and the first part of our relationship was extremely happy. She had a big heart, loved her daughters, was a great teacher and was very good with gifted kids.

She was, however, lugging around a whole bag full of issues from her childhood. It can hardly be a surprise that a woman has sexual hang-ups, anger issues and narcissistic tendencies when she grew up in a home where both parents were alcoholics; with her mum being a serial adulterer who lost a grand total of five husbands because of an inability to keep her legs shut. This was a woman who would drag her three young daughters out to bars on her weekend to have them, where they got to see mum at work getting free drinks as she identified her conquest for the night, after which the girls got to listen to their mum "perform" in the next room.

Her mum, somewhat predictably, ended up single and alone in a retirement complex, where she still managed to find ways to annoy other residents with her trademark selfish attitude toward everything.

Before long, it became clear that my wife's daughters ran the show and were both rude and ungrateful, having been spoiled all their lives. Both seemed unable to be faithful to a boyfriend; the older of the two slept with her boyfriend's roommates and best friends on more than one occasion. When I inquired as to when their mother would have a discussion with them about loyalty and faithfulness, she answered that they were just experimenting, and it was ok. I should have seen the signs.

I fell deeply in love with my new wife and wanted to make sure I was a better husband than I felt I had been before. Not long after we became serious, my business partners and I had a falling out - a long story - but it ended with me leaving the company and being left unemployed. I had money in the bank, but it wouldn't last forever. Having spoken with friends, I decided to form my own company, Osprey Group USA, with a UK branch run by some of my old army mates. The UK branch never panned out, but to my delight, Osprey Group USA was formed.

Time passed and in fairness, my issues must have played a part. I was still suffering the effects of PTSI without ever considering that I was, or that I needed help. I was a tough British Army Sgt Major, and I didn't need any head shrink holding my hand and telling me it would all be alright as long as I could afford to pay. On reflection– one of the worst decisions I ever made.

To add to my problems, the swinger lifestyle was common in my wife's family, with her younger sister and husband completely buying into the voyeur scene. From the outside, the swinger world seems like a dream come true, and for many is a sexy fantasy, but fantasies should remain just that. The truth is, fantasy and reality are two entirely different things. I soon discovered that my new wife got off on watching me flirt or have sex with other women. A dream come true, right lads! It wasn't too long before threesomes and foursomes had been tried, and while fun at the time, these only created suspicion and fed my own insecurities.

Everyone considers experimenting with sex, and as I said, the build-up or fantasies are powerful, but the reality requires either a very strong mutual trust or a total lack of love for your partner because, in reality, you are simply fulfilling your own needs. The other case is that you end up pandering to someone else's needs to fit in or out of the fear that you will lose them if you don't. My brother and sister-in-law at the time thrived on it and for them, it works, and who am I to judge? They are a great couple who are very welcoming. I enjoyed their company; we just never fully shared the same wants in life.

My reputation at work led to the signing of a long-term contract in the Middle East, one which would see me away for three out of every four months for the next three years; but with rock-star wages, it was a way to gain financial security in exchange for limited suffering and my wife not only agreed, but loved spending the money.

Now, don't get me wrong, there were a few guns I may have picked up that I'd always wanted, and I would always buy my team expensive gifts and use my wages to financially build the company. My wife was now driving a top-of-the-line Range Rover Sport to work and had absolutely no money worries. For the first year of my deployment, life seemed great; we spoke twice a day, once in the morning and once in the evening (the only time our schedules lined up), and I couldn't be happier.

It seemed, to all intents and purposes, that I had well and truly turned a corner in my life. I was building the company, building our financial security and providing for my family's needs.

I ended up paying for my eldest stepdaughter's college after her laziness and tendency to travel the world on other peoples' money cost her a scholarship and her biological father was smart enough to say no to her. They all got whatever they wanted as my income meant nothing was out of reach, and you'd better believe they made the most out of that! Cell phones were paid for, schooling, clothes, rent, flights across the country to attend a concert… you name it, I was paying for it. Whatever they asked for, they got, because my wife would never say no to them.

In fairness, she knew she was being manipulated, but her feelings of hatred towards her own mother meant she had developed a phobia of repeating the problem. She was desperate to avoid a situation where her daughters ended up hating her. Her way to compensate and placate them was to allow them to do as they pleased. I was raised to say thank you for everything, to have manners and to share with others. Our contrasting attitudes meant we often clashed on principle.

The deployment in the Middle East saw us take on more and more as the depth of the problem within the Jordanian military became crystal clear. I had the pleasure of working directly with the King's Office, with my immediate boss being another member of the senior Royal Family; a true soldier and man of outstanding integrity.

Prince Talal became known to my team as the Jordanian Sean Connery; not just for his looks, but for the stern demeanour he possessed that saw soldiers and officers alike run for cover when his motorcade pulled into the Sniper School. We also got to see the other side of a man in an important, public position in life, one who would turn up on an evening with a cooler full of ice cream and sit watching war movies with us until the early hours.

Prince Talal is a true gentleman whom I am honoured to say is a very close friend of mine, and if his family was ever threatened, I wouldn't hesitate to put a team together and go get them out.

We became involved in a lot more than we had originally signed up for, training and operationally, including retraining some of the Royal Family bodyguard teams, but it was a pleasure working for Prince Talal, so we didn't complain. We also added a lot of experience to our résumés fighting ISIS and assisting in keeping them out of Jordan.

Over the next year, things kept happening at home that raised red flags for me. As a result, I started to pay closer attention.

For example, I would come home and all of my shaving and washing stuff from my sink area had been put away, as if she lived there alone or was trying to create that image. When I asked, she said it was to help the house cleaner she now had to have, and even when I told her I didn't like it, she did it again when I left.

I had recently fitted security cameras inside and out, watching approach routes and the major access points to the house; a security measure I felt necessary after a life of upsetting terrorists. What they also gave me was the ability to watch my dogs from anywhere in the world. Being so far from home, I missed them, and the ability to see my home was always a nice, reassuring feeling that served as a reminder of why you were apart and what it was all for.

At first, she was all about the security, and then after a year, she started to complain about them and how she felt like a prisoner. I truly didn't see the issue at the time, because this was prior to her activities raising red flags. I soon realised, though, when she complained about me knowing when she left and came home, why it was bothering her. I knew when she finished work, and the time it took to drive home out of habit, and so without me realising, the cameras held her accountable.

At this stage, I did start to watch the cameras more, as her complaints had raised suspicion in me. This behaviour in me was driven in large part by my PTSI and its associated psychological impact. In particular, I suffered from a loss of self-confidence, a lack of self-worth and feelings of abandonment. This heightened my awareness of her actions and changes in attitude, so I started to pay a lot more attention.

Now look, I would never advise this as an option. The old adage of, "you never hear anything good about yourself when listening to others' conversations" is true, and often the only function it serves is to increase your anxiety and paranoia. All of this inflamed my latent PTSI issues, driving them to ever-greater heights. That said, time and again something felt wrong. Something was just not adding up and my sixth sense was screaming out to me.

It wasn't too long before I caught her talking to her older sister on the phone, saying, "No, don't worry, he can't see the texts because we use Viber-" this was followed by her looking at the camera mid-sentence and saying, "-hang on, I need to go outside. He could hear me..."

When I challenged her about this, it sparked a massive fight, one where I would be accused of not trusting her, of paranoia, keeping her prisoner, etc. To a degree, this had a ring of truth to it, and as she knew the history of Diane's death, more than once I was told, "No wonder Diane killed herself!"

Crushed, I let her convince me I was wrong, that it was all in my head, and I went back to the Middle East. Inside, however, something was screaming at me to keep looking.

One thing that caused me alarm happened on her 50th birthday. I knew I wasn't going to be there; she had already made it clear she was not delaying her celebrations until I came home. She also told me that she and her sisters were going to Palm Springs, a well-known swinger vacation and that I was not to ruin it with my paranoia.

It turned out to be more than just her sisters going, as her teenage kids went, as did my brother-in-law– all on my dime. I never cared about money and, to be honest, I never really have. If I have it, great! But if I don't, that's fine, so paying for the trip for everyone never really bothered me at the time.

To make her feel special, and to try and show her that I wanted her to have a good time, I ordered champagne and chocolate strawberries to be delivered to her hotel room every morning. You can imagine my surprise then when I got told off for interfering and that it was annoying, that it was my way of taking over.

As I've already explained, because of the difference in time zones, there were only really two times a day that we could speak; first thing in the morning and last thing at night. This was the highlight of my day, and any soldier who has deployed will tell you that speaking with home is a major morale boost. As my job deployment extended, there developed a noticeable resistance to calling me at those times, and I was often told that we don't need to speak every day.

Now, that may be true for some, but to me, my wife is my primary focus and I look forward to seeing her and talking on Skype or FaceTime. As a result, this caused me a great deal of hurt, leading to a great deal of friction and arguments between us.

I now know it was because she had been telling her "boyfriend" that we were all but separated, so speaking to me daily would somewhat ruin that narrative.

During her birthday weekend, we had spoken and she told me they were going to dinner, and that she would call after. Not only did she not call, but her phone was switched off and never came back on for 19 hours. None of her family answered their phones either, which was completely out of the norm.

"Absence of the Normal, Presence of the Abnormal!" These words once again rang around my head.

When she eventually did FaceTime, she had her older sister in the shot with her; both looking very guilty. No doubt she was there to provide backup to the story they had crafted; of how she'd drunk too much and had the worst hangover, and how her phone must have died while she was asleep. At that stage I never believed a word, wearing a mask of blissful unawareness, hiding my true suspicions. I suspected that her boyfriend was not only there, but that her family were all now meeting him, fully aware of and complicit in her cheating.

I have never confirmed this, but I have confirmed that she was sleeping with the guy for two years prior to this weekend - we had only been married for three - and from emails I would find, I knew her oldest daughter not only knew but supported the deceit, and if one knew, so did the other.

She had also been spending more time with her mother, whom she repeatedly professed she hated. This confused me, as every time she visited her, she came away depressed and angry. It never occurred to me until later that when you are doing something wrong, you often make yourself feel better by confiding in someone whose past says they will agree and encourage you, confirming to you that you are doing nothing wrong, and helping build your cover story of being the victim of a narcissist.

Seeing the words "We very soon realised we had the same sexual desires and decided to become fuck buddies when my husband was away," has a way of giving closure.

Towards the end of my contract in Jordan, I came home from the Middle East for Christmas. My son and his new partner were coming, and I was very much looking forward to it, but as I arrived home, I could tell immediately that something was wrong... It was clear from the moment I saw her at the airport. She gave quite the performance, but something was wrong. Her body language was off, her smile different.

We had the normal, passionate sex that night, but I noticed she had started to go straight to the shower immediately after we finished and had been for some time now. To my shame, I had cheated on my first wife and so was now recognising the signs of someone else cheating; late home from work, not wanting me to drive her to work or have lunch like we used to and dressing in sexier underwear than normal.

The following day we got into an argument, and she angrily accused me of being too aggressive in bed, and how it felt to her like I was "taking her back."

Now, that phrase wouldn't mean much to most, but I knew it was a common phrase my brother-in-law used to explain that, after the guy he just filmed shagging his wife had left, he would "take her back" by having sex with her, and it was a common action in the swinger world to take your wife back after she had sex with another person. I never challenged the phrase, but I did make note of it.

We also argued because I watched as she received a flirty text from a male teacher and accused her of what I suspected. She called the guy, who denied it, and I backed down. She called my bluff and was pretty cool about it. Time would tell me I was right; I had just suspected the wrong teacher... or I just never found proof of that one.

I also found my name was listed twice in the Viber App on her cell phone; one with my picture and one blank. I asked her to open it, and she swore to me that she had no idea what it was and that it was probably just a glitch. Being so desperate to prove to myself I was a good man and could be supportive, I backed down again as she accused me of not trusting her, revealing to me that she was thinking of leaving.

Hours later we got into it again, and she told me she wanted to separate. After a long conversation, she reversed her decision, telling me that she didn't mean it; that there was nobody else. I went for a walk to calm down and called my mum for a chat. During that call, my mum warned me to check my bank accounts, and although I told her my wife would never do that, I checked. On doing so, I discovered that she had just moved $50,000 into her account and then on into her daughter's account while I was on the phone with my mum.

Upon getting home, I challenged her, only to be confronted with, "It's my money too, I deserve it!" I told her she only had to ask, not just take it, and she calmed down and we left it unfinished. For the next hour, she acted in a way that was very compassionate and loving. This ended when I took my son to the shops.

This ended when we returned, and she was gone.

Back in the Dark

The cameras showed her immediately rushing to her phone as soon as we'd left before packing a bag in a frenzy and rushing out the door, getting into her car and driving away.

That was the last I was to see or hear from her for three months. She ignored my calls, texts and emails, leaving me totally in the dark as to what was going on. The only answer I received at that time was from her younger sister, who told me to just give her some space. I later saw a text from her older sister that said, "Don't get caught, get out now, I will come get you if I have to!"

So, the betrayal was as deep as I'd feared. Not only was she cheating on me, but her family all knew as well. On checking my company accounts, I found a very large amount of money unaccounted for, as well as sums of $5,000 frequently being moved to her daughter's account or being withdrawn every month. As my wife and company CFO, I trusted her and decided that it was not criminal. She was the company accountant; it was unethical, and I could take her to court on civil litigation, but in my head, I wanted her back. I wanted to save my marriage, I still loved her. On closer inspection, I found that she had moved cash for a long time, and I was too trusting to notice. She had also not sent money to my mum's account every month, as I had asked her to do.

The next three months were hell. She blocked me on everything. None of her family would answer me and I very quickly walked back into a dark place. My cousin, Jo, my best mate Tony and my friend Victor, were on speed dial for the entire period and helped keep me from believing all the accusations she had made about me to our friends.

Once again, I found myself collapsing inside; the embarrassment of my wife walking out, her comments about how she now knew why Diane committed suicide, accusations of being a narcissist and that I needed therapy, all tore away at me.

I found myself unable to stay in the house again. Agitation and a kind of claustrophobia took over, and I spent many, many hours walking the streets, talking to Tony, Jo and Victor on the phone, or just walking, locked away in my head, searching for answers. I had more than one "I'm done moment," and once again, my pups would never leave me alone long enough to reach the bottom of the spiral and I always put the gun down.

I had never been called a narcissist before, and to be honest, I didn't even know what one was, so I started therapy three times a week to find out if I was one and to cure it. It was during these sessions that I was to discover that I had been carrying around issues since I was 5-7 years old. On top of the issues of abandonment and a lack of sense of self-worth - feelings that I've highlighted in other parts of the book - I also discovered that an event that is still as vivid in my head as it ever was, an event that affected me more than I believed.

————————◆

It was a brisk winter's day. My best mate, Martin Drage, and I were out in the street playing, just as we would be any other day. I lived in the Paulsgrove area of Portsmouth at that time; a run-down area with prefabricated houses of World War II vintage, on a road called Newbolt Road.

Newbolt Road sat at the base of Portsdown Hill, overlooking the harbour and main city and was close enough to Portchester Castle - an old Roman fort on the ocean's edge - that the castle became my go-to playground. It wasn't unusual to see me there, fighting an imaginary enemy along the ramparts, dustbin lid shield and tree-branch sword, always winning, resulting in me being Knighted. "Sir Mark" was always my dream, and so I guess me ending up a soldier shouldn't have come as too much of a shock to my parents, although it seems I am in the wrong profession to be knighted nowadays. I would've had more of a chance if I'd learned to play the piano and sung at a few funerals than fighting for my country my whole life.

Newbolt Road had a fairly long straight stretch running from the shops and bus stops to the western end, bending downhill to meet the old Southampton Road at the eastern end. Martin and I had just bundled out of my house and, with no real plans, stood at the roadside. We both became aware of the roar of a car engine and, looking towards the shops, saw a small sports car hauling arse towards us.

Before I could even react, I remember Martin yelling, "I bet I can beat it!" as he took off towards the opposite side of the road.

Martin was not faster than the car.

Martin lost the bet as I watched my best friend get slammed at waist height. He was flipped up, spinning in the air like a rag doll as the sports car skidded out of sight to my left. I was transfixed with the image of my friend spinning in mid-air, falling, and yet almost following the sports car with the momentum of the hit, before landing face first and skidding along the road, travelling almost as far as the car took to stop.

I remember standing there, frozen, my young brain trying to take in what I had just seen. The road was full of our neighbours now, drawn out by the screeching of the car's tires. People were running over to Martin. A man was pulling the driver out of the car by his throat amid the frantic shouts of "Who has a phone?" Not everyone had a house phone back then.

I was awoken from my transfixed state by the sounds of a woman wailing and turning, I saw Martin's mum hysterically running back and forth across the front of our house. The next thing I remember was my mum stepping out from behind our hedgerow and smacking Martin's mum full up the side of her head with a frying pan, dropping it and catching the now stunned mother, dragging her into our house away from the scene before her on the road. As my mum reached our door, she shouted at me to follow, and I did.

I don't remember the ambulance arriving. I don't recall any sirens or bell noises, and I was sitting in the living room with a sugary cup of tea my mum made for me when a Police Officer walked in.

He terrified me! In his defence, he didn't mean to, and I would expect a certain level of shock had kicked in by then. He sat down, took out his notebook and proceeded to ask me a series of questions, the answers to some of which I just couldn't remember.

My mind was already in self-defence mode, blocking and locking away images that could harm me. I remember the officer becoming frustrated with me and me crying, to which my mum offered to use the frying pan on him if he didn't leave, and he beat a hasty retreat.

Martin survived the accident. I've no idea how, he was broken up pretty bad, but he did. He spent several months in hospital and was never really the same. He went off the rails as we grew up and we lost touch, but his failed race has lingered on in my mind.

———————◆

I had my suspicions, but I had let her convince me over and over that it was just paranoia and jealousy and that I was at fault - a key driver in my decision to undergo therapy - but things kept popping up that just didn't make sense.

I re-watched the video of her rushing out of the house more than once, analysing, looking for clues. After watching it a few times, I realised that one of the things she carried out was a bag full of wrapped Christmas Presents. This was odd; I hadn't seen those anywhere in the house.

I concluded that they must have been hidden; who were they for? The bag wasn't for her daughters. They had unwrapped all their presents from me; including a $1000 gift card each, knowing full well their mother was cheating and planned on leaving. They even had the cheek to return the day after she left to collect their money and presents, illustrating the selfish attitude of all three of them.

I started running scenarios in my mind. I reasoned that if she was at a hotel it would cost too much, and she was always tight with money. I concluded, therefore, that she must have had a bolt hole somewhere.

Over the next six months, her story unravelled, and it was confirmed that she ran to her boyfriend's house with stories of her lucky escape. He was to find out the depth of her lies a few weeks later. She spent the second half of the year playing the two of us; meeting me, speaking to me, even spending days and nights with me. Sex, promises of the future and how much she still loved me- just enough to keep me hanging on a thread.

All she needed was time to rebuild relationships with her mother and daughters, all of whom hated me as I stopped them manipulating her. As time passed and my therapy moved me toward a better place, I wanted her back and a chance to show her I had bettered myself.

I didn't care about the sex in the betrayal. She wasn't a virgin when I met her and we had dabbled in the world of swinging; it was the lies, skimming off money and the character assassination she enacted to friends and family to make her victim story believable that hurt most.

My PTS means some of the story was true, I'm not in denial of that and the work and therapy I have undergone has put me in a position where I am comfortable confronting that. I could be irritable, I did have a habit of wanting to stay home at weekends, procrastinating about honey-do's, all of which I was to find out were symptoms of undiagnosed PTSI. Like the best lies, these facts added a fraction of truth to her story of woe which lent credibility to the whole story, or at least enough to leave our friends undecided.

Throughout my life, there have been many times when I have heard a voice as clear as a bell in my head tell me something and, on one particular day, I heard something tell me to check her emails. I wondered if she had changed the password to her email, and so I checked. She had not.

I found the emails between her and another male teacher. The strange thing is that I actually came to feel fairly sorry for him. She was clearly using him, whereas it seemed apparent that he was truly in love with her.

At the time I discovered these emails, I had been going to therapy two to three times a week for almost six months. This therapy has helped me develop my mental strength, resilience and fortitude. For the first time in a long time, I felt happy, free from depression and had a sense of self-worth.

When I realised there was no rebuilding my marriage, I stopped going to therapy. To me, I was no longer depressed. I had proved to myself that I was none of the things she accused me of, and so I stopped going.

This was an error. One I would regret and one I would caution everyone about.

Reading the emails and monitoring them over the next few weeks was an intensely painful experience, but I wanted answers; I wanted the truth. Reading how your wife performs in bed from another man, or her describing their sex in graphic detail is not an easy thing to read.

It gets worse when you find a third person joining the conversion; another woman and a former college friend of his. She suddenly joined the conversation, and my ex-wife's desire to see her man with another woman had resurfaced and they are busy planning a threesome.

It wasn't long after this that things started to go wrong, and the emails changed in tone. He had obviously confessed his undying love for her; a love which she had rebuffed. He was just not her type; he was too weak and not manly enough. This I know because in the emails he complained after finding out she was still visiting me. She had told him in a previous conversation that "Mark rocks my world"; I'm sure that was painful for him to hear, and I shamefully admit to a level of satisfaction at his pain.

He pointed out that, in his opinion, I had wrecked her world as he replayed things she had told him about me as part of her process of gaining his trust and painting herself as a victim.

I watched as she rebuffed him over and over in the following days, telling him just enough to keep him where she wanted him, but always placating him with the same "I just need time" excuse. This compounded my sympathy for him. He had not only been lied to about me, but he had been lied to about how she felt and used him.

Even the third person, the new woman, kicked off at my ex when she asked her if she wanted to date the guy instead in one of the emails, as she wasn't looking for a relationship. This caused her to tear my ex a new arsehole over the way she was using him, telling her that he really loved her and that she was a bitch.

I fought the urge to email my agreement, agreeing that, yes, she is, but that would have ruined what was turning out to be quite the eye-opener, and I wanted enough evidence to protect my home and prove she was an adulteress. This turned out to be a pointless exercise. In Arizona, they don't care. If you can't agree on the division of property, it gets split 50-50, even if she had slept with the entire Cardinals football team.

She finally worked out how I was one step ahead of her and how I knew so much, but by then I had everything I needed, including emails between them both explaining how they only just got their clothes back on before the 5th graders walked in and caught them having sex on her classroom desk. I'm sure the district board and PTA would have had a field day with those emails, but I am not in the business of seeking revenge and have already forgiven her, which is why I have avoided using her name.

You may be asking; why has Mark included this story? How is this relevant to PTSI and his experiences with mental health? What do I get from this?

What this saga with my ex-wife shows is just how easy it is for the Darkness to find a way back into your life. It shows how easy it is for the Darkness to have an impact on the way you behave, act and respond to crises.

You don't have to be at war. PTSI can rear its ugly head and cause havoc at even the slightest moment of weakness. For me, PTSI, and my experiences in the military and with Diana devastated my sense of self-confidence and self-worth. Sure, professionally I knew my value; I went into business doing what I know I'm good at. Personally, though, my self-worth was completely shot. It led me to seek comfort in the wrong person.

Yes, she made me feel desired, at least in the beginning. This feeling is why I gravitated to her. She made me feel attractive, masculine, and desirable. This was good for me, good for my lost sense of self-worth.

When she cheated though, all of that shit came flooding back. My self-esteem evaporated. I blamed myself for the way she behaved, convinced myself it was my fault. As a result, my self-belief went too. I doubted my effectiveness as a man and as a husband; allowing her and her family to walk all over me.

My self-efficacy soon followed. I no longer believed that I was worthy of love and attention. I clung on desperately to the hope that she would come back, crippling me into place and making it impossible to envision a world in which I moved on for six long months. In that time, the only time I found comfort was those sporadic moments where she came back.

The cycle that feeds one's self-confidence relies on these things. With my self-confidence gone, the Darkness grew from a niggle to a clear voice, drawing me in ever deeper, convincing me that I no longer needed therapy.

I'm sure that those who work with her can put two and two together but only I can prove anything. And I won't. Who knows, they could have made up and be a couple now, and if they are, I hope, for his sake, they stay very happily married, although I have my doubts as to whether she is capable.

What I found in her emails was an exceptionally painful find; one I would not wish on my worst enemy. It was a find, however, that gave me closure. It gave me the truth. An irrefutable truth.

Everyone deserves the truth. People make mistakes, fall out of love or into lust with someone else, so just be honest. Be honest with yourself and with them. Let the person go without crushing them. Don't paint a picture to cover your own adulterous ways to the world in justification of your betrayal.

Do the right thing. Karma knows where everyone lives, and I have no doubts this was karma visiting me for the cruelty I dealt to my first wife through my own adultery. It does not matter how much you tell yourself, "it was my issues," "she never paid me enough attention," "we never had enough sex." The simple fact is, it is still never right to sleep with others and break hearts in the process.

Everyone has baggage. Everyone is fighting their own demons and we should always look to avoid adding to that.

I betrayed my first wife. I betrayed my friends. I am not proud of any of it. If I could change it I would, but I can't. All I can do is work to make myself a better man, a better husband, father, friend and boss, and to take the time to find out why I did the things I did. I can work to put them right, manage them, treat them so that I don't hurt anyone else.

Therapy has shown me why I did things, why I behaved the way I did. No, this doesn't make them right, and it certainly doesn't take away the pain I caused. What it does do though, is force me to take ownership, to take responsibility and admit to my failings. That has been the first step for me to be a better man, and I will continue to always strive to be a better man tomorrow than I was today.

It has also given me an inner strength that has better prepared me for struggles to come, ways to avoid the Darkness calling me back. I would be a liar, though, if I said the first six months of wondering where my wife was, trying to convince myself she was telling the truth and the general verbal attacks made against me and my character didn't have me very close to ending my life again as PTSI seized the opportunity to hit me like a steam train once again.

In truth, I don't doubt my wife loved me. I feel her own issues from her childhood and her mother's actions specifically left her with a cocktail of insecurities that she tried to overcome and leave behind. With these and her daughters' selfish ways, I think she just couldn't cope and slipped into old habits, unable to stop herself. Insecurities have far more power over you than you may think. I truly hope she is in a better place.

Chris

I have found over the subsequent years that depression is never far away when you are carrying baggage. This baggage may be something you are in self-denial about. It may also be baggage that you are unaware you are carrying, forced upon you by something that you are completely unaware has affected you as profoundly as it has.

One day you're happy, buoyant and seemingly fine, and then a song, a scene from a movie, a smell or a certain situation takes you to another place and time, and that involuntary, rhythmic clenching of your stomach starts as you try to suppress the urge to cry.

You see being alone as proof that nobody really cares and so; who would really miss you? Some friends reach out, aware that you may be struggling, but most are justifiably focused on their own lives and that's ok. To you, though, it's the start of another mental stream and the thoughts of "I'm annoying," "they're fed up with my moods," all begin to resurface and take over your psyche.

You start to feel that nobody wants you around because you are depressing, and you start to find reasons why you might be better off just ending it. One simple pull of a trigger, one bottle of pills; it will all stop. Most will tell you that "you just gotta get over it," or "keep yourself busy," which in itself says they have no idea what the symptoms of depression are. Procrastination, a total lack of drive and an inability to focus all mean that particular piece of advice, no matter how well it is intended, is useless to a depressed person.

To a depressed person, it just sounds like, "Oh shut up whining," and confirms to them that they are a burden. Society and its passion for labels, name-calling - especially if you disagree with the current media narrative - and the total hypocrisy displayed by media and politicians alike cannot help but be a factor in the growing number of suicides and mental illnesses present in the youth of today.

Veterans, many suffering in silence, watch as illegal immigrants are housed in hotels and given money to live on while they sleep on the streets, hungry and constantly shuffled and ushered on because they are unsightly. To them, suicide beings to look like an attractive choice, and grows more so with each passing day. They live in a country where it seems their sacrifice was all for nothing.

The "participation trophy" and "woke" brigade are slowly pulling the seams of normal society apart, weakening the fabric of resilience you need to survive in the world. Being punished for wrongdoing wasn't poor parenting or barbaric. It was teaching one of the most valuable lessons in the world; actions have consequences.

Every action has a consequence, and we see every day how people complain about what they are entitled to; "you can't do this or that," and "it's my right." Here's a little secret for you: you don't have any rights. If the majority agree with your wishes, you get it. If they don't, you don't. It's that simple. Don't believe me? Go to China, Iran or a multitude of authoritarian countries and demand your rights. you will learn very quickly that you don't have any.

Soldiers, police officers and first responders in general suffer to allow you the ability to complain and it's the general public's lack of understanding that leads so many to take their own lives as they are made to feel like a burden to the very public they defend. 22 PTSI-related deaths by suicide a day is an epidemic. The tragedy is that it's an avoidable one if we, as a society, care enough to learn, understand and support veterans and those affected by traumatic events. Until we do, it's only going to get worse.

————————◆

Chris turned out to be one of my best friends. We had similar backgrounds, professions and, most of all, a sense of humour. We had become friends when, along with his Commanders, he had attended a class I was teaching to assess my suitability to run some of their training.

Also present in that class was the only man I have ever kicked off a course. His résumé was somewhat sketchy to begin with, but the people I was working for were money-orientated, so they accepted his admission. He would turn up each day in a different colour flight suit and with different web gear, soon becoming the butt of a few jokes. His surname, Dick, never helped his cause.

One coffee break, while everyone was cleaning weapons, he piped up that he was writing a book about his life but was stuck on what to call it. Without missing a beat, Chris offered, "You should call it; 'How to be a Dick.'"

The place fell apart and even with everyone laughing, the jibe seemed to go right over his head. Needless to say, it started a barrage of suggested chapters, such as:

"I grew up a Dick";

"I've been a Dick all my life";

"How to be a complete Dick";

"The Life and Times of a Dick…" The list goes on...

The crux came when Chris and I were the observers on a stalk. The test is to move unseen towards the enemy, which in this case was us, and fire a blank shot, completely unseen. The rules are simple: if we see you, you fail.

We pretty quickly grew fed up with failing him and sending him back to the beginning, and so we just ignored him and focused on the guys who were actually putting the effort in. That proved harder than we expected as Dick was tiptoeing between cacti like Wile E. Coyote as if he had some invisibility cloak on! In all my years of training snipers, I had never seen anything like this - and neither had Chris - and we both lost it, giggling like teenage girls as this fool tip-toed towards us.

At the end of the day's training, I told the guy we would reimburse his money because I refused to train him any further. It was my belief that this skill just was not for him. In truth, I was more worried he would end up in a clock tower somewhere on a college campus and I didn't wish to be blamed for that.

From that point forward, Chris and I became very close friends. On leaving the military, Chris was coming to work with me at that Sniper School, but after Diane's suicide that was no longer an option as I refused to work there anymore. As it was, Chris found investors in Dallas, and Craft was formed.

Throughout our time at Craft, I warned Chris several times to lower his profile. He was a prime target for a revenge killing, but Chris was a larger-than-life character and wanted to please the investors, who clambered for stories of daring, stories that should have remained in a memory bank called opsec.

After I left the company, Chris reached out and we met in a bar in Las Vegas, where we had a very honest chat. He told me I was right and jokingly asked if I had any vacancies for him to join me again. We laughed, got drunk as we always did together, and I introduced Chris to another good friend of mine, Craig.

Craig was another Brit, a fellow sniper, who had to be rushed from his home in the middle of the night by the UK Counter-Terrorist Police as intelligence had alerted them to an attack planned against him. The police ambushed and apprehended the group responsible - complete with a video claiming responsibility for cutting his head off and all the tools of the trade in their car - as they were en-route to Craig's house. I had him tell Chris the story as I wanted to again warn him to lower his profile. Chris was suitably shocked at the story and promised me he would. I told him over and over; either terrorists or some nutter who wants to be the man who killed him would turn up to do the job. I told him to be careful.

We parted and promised to speak more often as you do with most friends. We did keep in touch, and it was always funny when I'd get a text that just said "wanker," to which I always replied, "Fuck off Popeye."

The call that came at five in the afternoon made me feel physically sick. Not just the news, but also the utter guilt for being right. Chris had been shot multiple times and killed on the shooting range we used to teach at, and by a so-called PTSI suffering former Marine Chris was trying to help.

Familiar feelings of guilt and responsibility filled my mind. Why did I not pester him more to lower his profile? We'd already received death threats from the Middle East that saw both of our homes patrolled by SWAT patrols, so why had he not taken that as a warning? Why did he allow somebody so close to him to catch him off-guard?

Chris and his friend Chad died that day, and my friend was gone. The man who dropped everything to be at my side when I lost Diane, who gave up his leave to take care of my dogs, picked up my Mum and Son from the airport. Gone.

I sat down, numb, memories flooding my mind. Memories of the times we would fight each other, both getting split lips more than once. The fights we got into in bars because we were both having a bad PTSI day or because Chris was just a good guy and saw one of our mates getting sucker-punched and we both jumped in.

Never again, he was gone.

On the day of Chris's funeral, my flight was running late and it looked as though I would miss the public ceremony. I had warned the guys waiting for me and, to my surprise, as soon as the plane doors opened, Dallas PD officers stepped aboard, instructed everyone to remain seated and escorted me from the plane and to a waiting police car. They took my luggage ticket and said they would bring me my bag and rushed me to the stadium. I can never thank those officers enough for what they did for me that day.

I didn't go down onto the Dallas field with others close to Chris; I was there to say goodbye to my mate, and from where was not important. I sat, staring at his coffin draped in the American flag, almost unable to believe my mate was inside it. I listened to Taya with tears in my eyes, to his teammates who had served with him and to one person, unable to stop his ego, tell three lies about his relationship with Chris. Then I left with a former Air Force pilot and friend, to join other friends in an evening of toasting Chris.

The following day was something I will never forget. It was a horrible, cold, wet day that seemed to match the mood of many as we set off to join the funeral column for the drive from Dallas to Austin. It is no exaggeration to say that, during the entire two-hour-plus drive, there was not one bridge or stretch of interstate that was not lined with Texans saluting their son on his final journey. It was a day I will never forget.

I have watched various journalists attack Chris, branding him a liar, or even a murderous man, and on more than one occasion I have typed and then deleted a reply to these people, as I realised they wouldn't understand or care.

Needless to say, Chris was an amazing patriot, a man who would have given his life defending anyone, and who was not a liar. One incident that has been called a lie was Chris being mugged at a gas station.

Some say that there's no evidence and it didn't happen. Well, I was in Dallas with Chris that day and in his home working on lesson plans when I took a call from him immediately after the event. I was also with him that night, when, at an event, a senior Dallas official walked up to us and said, "Chris, can I have one day when you're not in trouble," and we all laughed.

Chris is not a liar. There have been many times since his passing that his grin; the one that usually meant somebody was about to get choked out, just popped, crystal clear into my mind's eye, just before something stupid happened to me and I could see and hear him laughing. He got on well with Diane. They both had the same sense of humour, and I have no doubt they are having fun messing with me about now, and that's the way I have chosen to remember them. Two good souls, taken way too soon, and with more issues than they would ever let on. Brave and yet foolish at the same time.

Seek help. Don't become someone's happy memory way before your time.

PTSI- An Unwanted Guest

L iz was a rare gift from God. A truly loving soul who walked into my life unexpectedly one afternoon while visiting friends. She was the type of girl who just makes you gasp; radiant, beautiful and with an air of grace that concealed her own lack of self-confidence. I didn't know that, or care, at that moment. All I could think was why can't I find someone like her?

As I explained in the opening of this book, my life had all but collapsed around me for the second time in a fairly short period and had brought me all the way back to a very dark and silent place; a place I had spent considerable time in before. A place where nothing penetrated; reason, hope, love, responsibility... nothing, just Darkness.

A Darkness that beckons, reasons with you that it is your best option and salvation. A Darkness that camouflages itself as a path back to light. Trust it and it will ease your pain, remove your burdens and free you again, never mentioning that the price is to ruin the lives of so many others. Those you leave behind who will never truly know why you did it, and who will tear their own lives apart looking for the answers.

It was for this reason that I finally looked for help and found a therapist to whom I could relate. The catalyst was when my estranged wife had called me a narcissist, psycho and a son of a bitch. She was so convincing that I felt compelled to do something about it.

My therapy helped me identify issues I had carried from childhood and how they had shaped my young brain to react to certain situations. I found I had issues with feelings of "I'm not good enough," a "fear of being shamed" and "fear of abandonment" from women, all of which drove me to an amazingly successful career but absolute failure as a husband and father.

The reasoning for these issues came out in tearful collapses during therapy sessions and made me realise that trained therapists are a lot like military interrogators insomuch as they know just how to walk you into a corner where you have no choice but to face the truth before you. I noticed that THERAPIST actually breaks down into "The Rapist," and I left the office more than once feeling ashamed and violated. Having to admit you are not superman is quite the shock.

My issues, as it turns out, were created by three incidents in my younger years that, while I didn't feel it at the time, caused me considerable trauma. The first was the cause of my "Fear of Abandonment."

My mum, like many at the time, worked hard to make ends meet. As a result, she needed a child-minder for me during the day. Not far from our house was an older lady who fostered children and provided day-care for others, and it was here that I was deposited every day.

As far as I can remember I was around four or five years old at the time. All I could remember of this period is the dark outline of a woman who I still have a lingering feeling of fear over. I couldn't remember any specific details about her or the other kids, just a feeling of pure dread when I think about that house and of being scared all day. The incident, if you can call it that, came out when my therapist asked me to think of my first memory as a child, and before I could reason why, I was in tears explaining my memory.

One morning after my Mum had dropped me off, a moment I dreaded daily, I knew my Mum would pass the house on the bus and so I snuck out to the front yard and waited. I was already upset at being left there and so, when the bus passed and I saw my Mum, I was already in floods of tears.

My Mum saw me, jumped off at the next bus stop, not far down the road, and ran back to see what was wrong. My joy at seeing my Mum coming was short-lived. When I explained that I didn't want her to go and I hated it there, I got my legs slapped by a very angry Mum, who pointed out that my stupidity had now made her late for work.

I was crushed as she marched me back inside. It is at this point that my memory hits a blackness that, try as I may, I simply cannot recall. My therapist took a deep breath in and just said, "Abandonment."

"You were abandoned by the one woman you saw as your world and safe zone, and that traumatised your young brain." Who would've known that one incident could set you on a path that would cause such pain to someone you love and who had done nothing to hurt you?

The next issue was also discovered in my first period of therapy when she asked, "What is the first memory of your dad?"

Again, I had no hesitation and the memory burst out. I was again aged between five and seven years old and most of my cousins, aunts and uncles were over our house. We had a large and very close family, something of a local mafia if truth be told, but I remember beer flowing and everyone joking as was always the case.

My dad was always my hero; a soldier before me and a man I constantly sought approval from, and so I tried to make a joke and impress him. It went horribly wrong for me, and it ended with my dad playfully kicking me up the arse, all my uncles and aunts laughing, and me running off up to my room, humiliated and crying.

My mum found me and was furious with my dad. Now, he never meant to shame me, but that event was to ignite a deep-seated fear of being shamed that led to me being far too concerned with what everyone else was thinking of me instead of those closest to me.

Everything comes in threes I was told, and this is no exception. The last and most damaging issue I never discovered until I returned to therapy when my actions had pushed Liz, my wife, away from me to a point where we separated.

I had stopped going to therapy the first time when I found out the truth about my estranged wife and because I had proved I was nothing she had accused me of. The fact that she was doing all she had accused me of and deflecting it back at me was all the validation I felt I needed.

My wife at the time had accused me of being too restrictive, controlling and accusing her of cheating all the time. In fact, some of that would turn out to be true as a result of my third issue. I had decided to begin therapy to prove that I was not a narcissist and to try and win my wife back by changing from the man she had spent two years telling all our friends I was.

The therapy helped me immensely and I was so pleased to be able to tell my wife how well I was doing and that we could start again. She kept telling me she needed time, maybe a year, maybe less, to sort out her relationship with her daughters. This didn't stop her calling, texting and visiting once a month to sleep with me. At the time, I saw this as progress, but time showed that it was just a well-calculated plan to keep me from finding the truth.

To me, I was not depressed; I had proved to myself I was none of the things she accused me of, and so I stopped.

This was an error and one I would caution everyone about. Depression and PTSI can often appear gone but more often than not it is still lurking in the dark, waiting for a trigger.

The trigger was my greedy and jealous ex-wife, who, when she discovered that I was happy and in love with Liz, demanded that the final part of the divorce settlement be completed, even though she had agreed to give me longer just a few weeks before. In the settlement, she had secured equity from my house, and to pay her I would have to refinance, take her off the deed and pay her $50,000 from a house that was never hers. When she found out about Liz, I received a letter from her lawyer giving me 30 days to prove the house was on the market or pay her the money.

This was to be the shock and trigger that placed me on a downward spiral and led to me making Liz's life unbearable as my issues raised their ugly heads, and my PTSI gave them the fuel to run riot.

PTSI is an extremely damaging illness and one that still carries a significant social stigma. It is not a soldier's illness, although the lives soldiers lead makes them more susceptible to it. It is an illness that affects millions. Trauma, and traumatic situations, can happen anywhere to anyone.

I am by no means a doctor or expert on PTSI, but I have spent vast amounts of time researching it. It is in my nature to want to know all I can about an enemy. I have been trained that way.

In short, it shuts down the frontal lobes of your brain, the parts where reasoning and logic dwell, leaving you with the "old brain"; the first part of the brain that forms, where emotions and "fight or flight" lives. Obviously, this is not a good place to be making day-to-day decisions from.

To a sufferer, it seems like the world is against them. They simply cannot understand why people do not see things like them or understand them. This is because they are seeing an almost alternate version of events, expanded by issues that already cause them pain that they may be totally unaware of, such as feelings of abandonment, shame and the internal perception that they are not good enough. Not being able to see mental issues or the chemical imbalance it can cause often leads to anxiety, panic attacks and suicidal thoughts, as depression paints your world inky black. I believe it's the lack of understanding and the feeling of not being able to get people to see why you are the way you are that has led to the 22 veteran suicides a day that we now suffer.

This book is about my failings, the people I have hurt, let down, and how something can lead to a successful career and yet at the same time rob you of the one thing you have looked for your entire life... Love.

I also wish to reiterate that the words in this book only describe events as seen through my eyes and so it may vary considerably from how those involved saw it and that's ok as well. The only way to learn, to grow, is to see life, to see you through the eyes of others as well as your own.

Liz is incredible. She brought a love and happiness to me I had never known, not fully, not in this way. She never, ever noticed another man in the room or gave anyone the impression she had any interest in anyone but me, and yet I was to all but drive her away and hurt her in a way I truly never intended because I was too proud and stubborn to see that I was not fixed. I was not ok and unbeknownst to me, I was once again spiralling down.

Opening the letter from my ex's attorney chilled me to the bone and sent me into an almost immediate cold sweat panic attack. Where was I going to get $50,000 from in a month?

All I could see was the failure I was: losing a home in front of my new wife, not being good enough and no doubt losing her to another. I never once saw how much she loved *me*, not the house, not my reputation and not my potential. She loved me, just me and she stood by me and was my strength throughout that and the following stress.

I nearly fucked it though. I couldn't see how I was pushing her away with my anger, fear and conviction that I wasn't good enough for her and would invariably lose her. My biggest fears combined and, fuelled by PTSI, were the issue. Not Liz… Me.

The source of my biggest fear never came to light until I returned to therapy, and I was asked what event has caused my all-encompassing belief that I would always fail to be enough and that someone would take the girl I loved. I have been old-fashioned, for want of another definition, since before I can remember– an uncontrollable romantic and true believer in "happy ever after," and so every time I have fallen in love, I have fallen 100% and believed it was forever… Right up to the moment that my fear finds evidence that life is going to hurt me again; evidence that, every time but once, was wrong. I was asked by my therapist where these feelings could have stemmed from. after thinking on the question for a few moments, it came flooding back, complete with music.

———————◆

When I was 16, my best mate and I would be out down the seafront every night in my hometown of Portsmouth. Nobody carded anyone in those days, as we had our own "local" pub and were frequently drunk.

My hometown of Portsmouth was a haven for foreign students visiting the UK and as young boys do, we very quickly found out that French and Italian girls were way more forward than Brits. The rule was, whomever a girl showed the most interest in, the other made an excuse and left them alone and, in one case, I was glad that Kev was the lucky one.

We had met a French girl who spoke very little English, but she was clearly very taken with Kev. As per the rules, I made an excuse and headed for the walk home. I was very close to home, some two miles away when I became aware of somebody running up behind me and turning was surprised to see Kev barrelling his way towards me. I blasted him with questions about why he was done so fast, did he get anywhere, and so on. During his answers, it became clear that her lack of English had become an issue, and that trying to politely sign "do you want a fuck?" got too embarrassing and so he settled for a cheeky wank, as that was much easier to convey via gestures.

As I was congratulating him, I couldn't help but notice that he was limping and seemed to be in considerable pain? He was reluctant to explain at first, but eventually explained that she was a little inexperienced, and had pulled back and forth on his fun-stick like she was pumping water out of the Titanic! She then mistook his moans of pain for pleasure, and proceeded to move into ramming speed, splitting his foreskin in the process! Barely suppressing my laughter, I asked why he didn't stop her, to which he said he didn't want to complain as he was still hoping for more and was worried she would say no! I laughed the rest of the way home while he limped and begged me to stop.

It was on one of these "forays" that we saw a gorgeous girl standing alone outside Southsea Pier. This time, I was the chosen one and Kev made his excuses. In short, this girl was to become my first wife and mother to my two children, maybe sooner than I had planned, but I've never claimed to be smart.

She invariably met and became friends with my best mate Kev, and the three of us would hang out together all the time. I never had a single jealous or suspicious bone in my body and had fallen hopelessly in love. There was a well-known nightclub on the seafront called *Johanna's*, notorious for being full of sailors and where the doormen never cared if you were 18 or not.

One night we were all having a good time there and it was my round, so I suggested that they dance while I got the drinks in. While at the bar, the song *Vienna* by Ultravox came on, a slow song and one most would slow dance to. Without a care in the world, I looked towards the dance floor to plan my route back carrying three drinks and as I looked the crowd parted and my heart dropped to my stomach.

There they were; slow dancing. I could almost forgive that; we were pissed, they were friends and it was that sort of song. It was the fact that she was running her fingers through his hair and caressing his neck that immediately made me feel sick to my stomach. Even at that age, I knew it was a very intimate thing to do and my heart was broken at this betrayal by the two people I loved and trusted the most.

We argued, I was told I was mistaken and overreacting, but the damage was done and very soon I stopped seeing Kev. Our friendship was destroyed, and to this day I have never spoken to him.

I am unable to listen to that song even now without it taking me back to *Johanna's* and that betrayal. About 8 months into our relationship, where we never spent a day apart, she became pregnant and back then it was abortion or marriage, and after much arguing between parents, we were married. I never fully trusted or forgave her and used it as an excuse to myself when I would cheat on her multiple times later in our lives.

She was a fantastic mother, who, due to my constant deployments, raised our children almost single-handedly, and I am very proud of them all. She never deserved the way I betrayed her, my fears and inability to trust her fully were never justified, and neither was any excuse I gave myself for cheating on her. I have no doubts that my betrayal and our constant time apart pushed us further apart until we really had nothing left in common, and we divorced just before I finished my Army career. She is a kind loving person; an amazing mum and I am truly sorry I hurt her in the way that I did. We both met at a very young age; she already had issues from a terrible childhood and I was carrying my own insecurities and so, becoming parents before your 17 birthday with all the trouble that caused, we had an uphill battle from the start.

Rights Don't Exist

W hen Liz tried to tell me I was driving her away, all I heard was drama and exaggeration and I dismissed it out of hand or said whatever she needed to hear to stop the argument. In my head, I was right and she was wrong

On the day she told me she needed time away from me, and she told me exactly why, she listed my actions and for the first time, I could see she was right. I never had a leg to stand on. My issues had caused me to lose my temper, shout at her, accuse her of cheating, twist every argument until it was her fault and demand 90% of her attention.

As much of an arse as I was, she'd stood by me and loved me until she couldn't do it anymore. It was a wake-up call I will never forget. She was the one person I never, ever wanted to hurt, and I had let her down and hurt. She loves as hard as I do, and the man she trusted and believed in had turned her world inside out. Therapy was to show that Liz also had issues that she was carrying, and this added to her depression, and while it was comforting to know it was not all me, the part I had played still left me falling back into Darkness.

I am the first to admit that I felt PTSI was just one of those "cry baby" excuses that was best remedied with a large mug of man the fuck up, and I guess I was most definitely a part of the problem. It is both wrong and right the way the Military moulds soldiers. After all, to be able to motivate a man to stand up and charge when the rock he is safe behind is being peppered by bullets takes a certain mentality and self-belief. This courageous mindset is also one of the reasons we continue to lose 22 veterans a day to suicide.

Towards the end of my career, I began to see a new attitude to mental illness, one where soldiers were encouraged to speak up, seek help and not feel stigmatised by it. Whilst this was a turning point, everyone still knew that if you did you had endangered any chance you had of a successful career.

While that sounds unfair and harsh, soldiers are not issued tickling sticks, they are issued rifles, bayonets and grenades and expected to unleash hell on an enemy, day or night. To that end, a Junior Commander who has displayed symptoms of stress or requested therapy is, without doubt, going to cause his Commanders to question his ability to lead without crumbling or a relapse. They have no choice; the lives of other men and women are at stake, so by default, soldiers who seek help with a mental issue label themselves and call into question their ability to deal with the tremendous levels of stress associated with combat deployments.

It remains the same today, it has to, and so we are still watching as soldiers avoid help, bottling everything up and "soldiering on," which invariably means that when they leave the safety of all they have known and attempt to re-join society, they often find themselves isolated and alone in a world that just does not understand them. A world that has never seen the levels of evil man is capable of first-hand or is even accepting of the way they approach everything with a "can do" attitude, believing that anyone who complains is a whiny fuck.

Every soldier knows that the mantra, "Don't give me problems, give me solutions," is normal... isn't it? Sadly, it is not to most civilians. I don't mean that in a derogatory way, just that most civilian jobs do not have death as a consequence of failure as a key consideration.

They say that hindsight is 20-20. Looking back, I can clearly remember many of my men and friends who needed help at various times in their career and who bottled it up where, in some, it sits just waiting to explode. In others, it has manifested as temper or fury, ending in a fight that led to their arrest or becoming a career stopper. I can see now that some of the "grumpy" or "crazy" types in the Army were actually very much in need of help; a help they never knew they needed because their world tells them to "man the fuck up soldier."

My early career was something of a meteoric rise to the top. I wasn't with the Reserves for long before joining the regular Army, and I went from Private to Sergeant in a little over 5 years, a speed that generated significant professional jealousy and made me a lot of enemies. Jealousy and back-stabbing are part and parcel of an alpha-male society, and so it didn't come as a surprise when not everyone was happy about my promotions.

That said, I had proved myself by gaining top student awards or high grades in all that I did. My desperation to prove myself as good enough in my dad's eyes drove me on at work, but had the opposite effect in relationships, where a constant need for affirmation kept swinging me on a pendulum that has lasted until this day. This is a pendulum that has self-destruction at one end, and a happy, normal life at the other.

I was the father of two when I finished British Army Basic Training at the ripe old age of 20, and while I was "old" for Basic Training, I most certainly was not ready to raise other humans. I was blessed with a woman who is still an amazing mother to our children, who while fighting her own demons from before we met still managed to raise a son and daughter that I am immensely proud of.

I joined Basic Training having served in both the Infantry and a specialised unit and so arrived almost fully trained and fully fit. For me, the hardest part of the training was being away from my wife and kids. I loved them all very much and it was the burning pain you feel in your gut of missing them that caused me the most anguish.

The actual Army bit was a doddle; I loved being a soldier, I loved the constant challenge, and I was driven on by the knowledge that my dad would be proud of me at last. The stupid thing was, my dad had always been proud of me and things my mind saw as rejection were nothing of the sort and I was never to truly realise that until it was too late.

Basic Training is the first time you discover that the friends you make in the Army are unlike any you have met before. A shared love of the job, a shared suffering and the manner in which the Army breaks your soul and rebuilds you the way they need you, all combine to give you friends for life; friends who would literally die for you and you for them.

Now, some may recoil at the statement of the Army breaking you. You may feel it inhuman, devoid of basic rights or cruel. I have seen some say the military is racist, and while some individuals are, the military itself is the most non-racist society you could ever be a part of. The Army was simple; you were either a good soldier or a bad soldier and the colour of your skin, social background or wealth had fuck all to do with it. I remember later in life, talking with the father of a young Fijian soldier at his Passing Out Parade, who asked me if his son would face prejudice in the British Army. My reply wasn't what he was expecting.

I told him if he was asking if his son would be called a black fucker at some stage, then the answer was yes, and it may well be me as his Sgt Major. His wide-eyed response and the fact that, like most Fijians, he was built like a brick shithouse and looked like he had a punch with the power of a steam-driven piston, convinced me that I should hasten to explain.

In the Army, when you fuck up or annoy a JNCO or SNCO, the most obvious feature about you was suddenly going to become the focus of any response or suggested recovery from whatever travesty you had committed to draw their anger in the first place.

By way of example, if you had a big nose, "Oi, Pinocchio, you big nose fucker," was probably going to the opening line of the one-way conversation. If you were overweight, "Oi, balloon boy, you fat fucker," was probably a good bet, and so if the colour of your skin made you stand out, it was probably going to feature in the opening line.

I also pointed out that if his son was called that every time he was spoken to, then he needed to report it immediately. That is racism and 90% of soldiers simply will not stand for it. The man who saves your life in combat is your brother, irrespective of his skin colour, and soldiers know that.

Through my explanation, his demeanour softened, he laughed and bought me a pint. This response is a by-product of the toughening process the Army instils into you that at the time you do not see, but as you experience deployments you start to realise is necessary.

The acceptance of verbal insults, humiliation or aggression subconsciously prepares you to face the true horrors of what man is capable of, from close quarters hand-to-hand killing through to surviving capture and interrogation. This is, in my opinion, a much-needed part of building a soldier.

A soldier's ability to suffer pain, humiliation or visual horror and then get back up, motivate himself or others and return to the fight is essential. Trying to apply civilian "woke" ideas to a society whose sole function is to kill and destroy upon command is the beginning of the end for the Western world and for liberty and freedom.

Now, soldiers are not cold killers. In fact, most soldiers hate the thought of war, especially those who have seen it, but they are better educated than many would believe. Not only are soldiers operating some of the world's most advanced technology - even the fighting Infantrymen - but they are generally much better informed and aware of global current affairs, the risk and reward of political actions and the need to hold the line of freedom from those who would take it from you.

Many people have no idea what soldiers do or think and just dismiss them. Many will say that they never asked for anyone to defend them, but are totally unaware that without soldiers, our enemies, physical and corporate, would overrun our accepted lives to make the world the way they want it.

The soldier's biggest strength is also his biggest weakness in Western society; his loyalty and honour, because their respect for orders and government will often lead them to allow self-promoting politicians to act in a way that is detrimental to society. That deep-seated honour and integrity hold them in barracks when maybe they should act in defence of the people they serve.

Our enemies' soldiers do not have that; they will crush anything and anyone at their politicians' directive as they do not possess the freedom of thought. They have been indoctrinated with religion, communism or a repressive political ideology for their entire lives and so the weakest part of democracy is its people.

If I can get you to vote in a certain way, then I don't have to fight you. That is why every democratic election is interfered with by religious or communist-controlled governments worldwide as the preferred method to wage war. War is now a balance between supporting unseen acts like cyber-warfare and plausible deniability to avoid good old-fashioned combat.

For this very good reason, the military is forced to create a certain mindset to allow for such large bodies of men and women to function as one unit. If you start with the whole "my rights" nonsense, it quickly falls apart and we will all lose our freedom.

Soldiers already know that "Human Rights" are a myth perpetuated by politicians for personal gain. In truth, the only reason you have any rights is because the majority agree that they are needed.

If the majority decide tomorrow that people of Asian origin should be jailed, they will be hunted down just as Jews were in Nazi Germany, with all their rights stripped in a moment. If you doubt that, look at how fast looters rob stores, Police get assassinated in their cars, racist elements like BLM and ANTIFA gain support from so-called mainstream civilians, indoctrinated by owned media and ask again if it's truly so far-fetched.

So, telling soldiers all about your rights will probably invoke humour and sarcasm, because they have seen just how many rights people around the world do not have, and that hiding behind a shield of words and demands has never deflected a bullet.

In our current society, where names and labels, division and hatred are being manipulated for personal gain by the upper echelons of society, veterans find themselves even more isolated at the incredible lack of vision or understanding being displayed by the majority of society at the behest of power games of greedy politicians. Throw in the effects of PTS and 22 a day seems like a success.

My fear for the country, and the Democratic Western world in general, is that "woke" generals and "woke" recruiting campaigns will set the USA and its allies up for defeat in any conflict with a brutal totalitarian regime like China or Russia.

China still builds their soldiers to respect winning at all costs and indoctrinates the fanatical belief that the country comes first, and against that system, "woke" doesn't work, rights don't exist, and you become the vanquished.

The military is the best at slowly stripping individuals of their ideals and beliefs while installing their own versions. It has to be this way, and while I can almost feel the wave of objection as I write this, it still remains a fact.

A weak military means defeat, and the best-equipped military in the world is useless if it is staffed by "woke" sycophants who have no stomach for true warfare. For this very reason, the military trains the way they train because it is not only a proven route to victory, but it is a requirement.

Defeat is not an option. Society is not equal, we are not all the same and people who want to work in the medical field or in IT are not generally the same as people who grow up watching war movies and wanting to be knights in shining armour, AND THAT'S OK!

We are not all the same. We may well have been created by God in his image, by aliens in their image on behalf of God or developed from frog spawn - who knows - but we are NOT all the same, and for good bloody reason. I believe creation or evolution, whichever floats your boat, designed us to fill specific roles.

Look at nature. Look at large, informed communities in nature. Ants, termites and bees have workers, a hierarchy and a military, and they have specific biologically programmed roles and attitudes. We are the same no matter what "woke" types wish to believe, and even the most liberal woman in the world becomes a violent threat when her children are threatened; nobody messes with Momma Bear! It's inside us all, it's just some are better suited to that role in society.

The kicker is that warrior ants don't retire or have to fit back into society whereas humans do, and it is at this juncture that the military fails spectacularly. If the military spent as much time reintegrating soldiers back into society as they do inducting them into the military way of life, I believe suicides would become a thing of the past. Once again though, it comes down to budgets and the military does not control their budgets– politicians do.

Londonderry

One incident I was to find affected me far more than I believed happened during a deployment to Londonderry - Derry to the Catholics - when I was a very young Platoon Sergeant. I had been promoted very quickly and I was to find it made me a lot of enemies in the men whose careers I jumped.

I was deployed with my multiple; a patrol of 12 men, to monitor the perimeters of the anniversary parade for Bloody Sunday, a controversial incident that is still the subject of intense debate; an incident where British Paratroopers returned fire, resulting in the death of multiple civilians.

Londonderry is an old city and still has the old city perimeter wall in place; more of a tourist attraction nowadays, but it has a large monument and multiple cannons still in place along the walls. This high ground overlooked the Catholic housing estates of the Bogside; a notorious stronghold for the IRA, and from here every year, senior police officers would stand and watch the parade.

My orders dictated that I report to those officers at 4 p.m. to see if they had any additional tasks for us. I halted my patrol just short of the street that led to the wall and told the Commanders to position the men under cover until I returned.

There were complaints from the lads who wanted to get a look at the parade, but it was not tactically smart to expose them all on the top of the city ramparts, and so myself and LCpl Roberts, a.k.a Robbo, patrolled down to the officers and reported to the senior officer on-site.

He told us he had no more tasks for us but asked to borrow my rifle to use the optic to view the crowd and I passed it to him. He scanned the crowd for a few minutes and passed it back, apparently satisfied that all was well.

We were about ready to return to the lads back on the street when my attention was grabbed by the sound of synchronised footsteps from the crowd. I looked back toward the crowd to a terrifying spectacle. The entire parade had started marching on the spot and then, under the direction of the parade marshals (all IRA men), they all turned as one to look directly at us. The crowd was some 275 meters away, but there was no doubt they were looking straight at us. Just as I felt a chill of danger, A bright flash erupted to my left, and I barely had time to think "shit, bomb!" before the world went black.

The next memory I have was opening my eyes, lying flat on my back, surrounded by a strange, deafening silence. As I looked up at the dust blotting out the sky above me, my training kicked in and I immediately wiggled my fingers and toes to check they were still there and grabbed my fist mic:

"Zero, this is 31 Bravo! Contact, Bomb! Casualties wait out!?"

The first thing any competent Commander does is call in the incident so that assistance can be immediately mobilised. All you provide is the very basics that the ops room will need while you, as the Commander, assess the situation and send a detailed report.

With my sense of dread growing, I could hear the chilling sound of moaning from the direction of the 12 or so officers that were placed around the monument at the time of the blast. With a pang of realisation, I became aware of the pained screaming from a voice I knew; Robbo, my Corporal. I jumped to my feet and hurtled toward the sound, where I was greeted with the sight of him buried under concrete slabs blown from the monument. I started hauling them off of him until one large section remained.

I braced myself, tearing my hands to pieces as I tried with every ounce of strength I had, but I just couldn't budge it. I looked around frantically for some help and screamed at the three or four police officers who were standing nearby, frozen and numbed by shock.

"Get the fuck over here now!" The shout sparked them into life, and as they helped me heave off the final slab, my radio cut into life and the pilot of the Army Lynx helicopter that was video recording the parade, had seen the blast and heard my subsequent Contact Report, told me that he was going to land in the car park 150 metres to my left to collect casualties.

Directing others to assist, we carried Robbo to the car park. In what was a truly courageous piece of flying, the Lynx came straight down with only a few feet of clearance between his blades and the buildings; an example of truly masterful flying and a clear indication as to the risks that a soldier will go to in order to save a brother.

With Robbo on the Lynx and having briefed the crew on his injuries, they took off and I headed back on patrol with my multiple to assess the damage and assist in the recovery of any further casualties.

I'm not entirely sure how much time had passed, but I was tapped on the shoulder by one of my Corporals who told me Zero (base) had been calling me repeatedly on the radio. I had heard nothing.

They had told me to go firm; Army speak which meant to stay where I was. They had only just realised that I was shoulder-to-shoulder with Robbo and so very possibly injured.

My frustration and anger grew and, at some stage while we waited, I walked off alone. A soldier alone in a catholic/IRA stronghold is in grave danger, and my rash decision to walk off was a poor one. I found myself in an adjacent road, drawing the attention of four to five men who started chucking verbal abuse my way.

Wrong day, wrong man. I removed my helmet, dropping it in a doorway to my left and placed my rifle in the doorway with it. I returned the favour, calling across to the fuckers, telling them to try it if they thought they were up to it when a muffled shout from my right sent them fleeing down the street and round the nearest corner.

I looked in the direction of the shout and saw Dave A, a good friend of mine, march down with his own multiple. He told me he was there to get me off the ground, and I was soon in an armoured vehicle heading back to base.

Back at base, I was examined by the Medical Officer; our unit doctor, who found the only physical injuries were deafness; which was correctly assessed as temporary, and my upper body looked like Mike Tyson had used me as a punching bag. Apart from that, I was fine.

That's the thing though, physically I was ok. That's easy to spot and easy to assess. What is often overlooked is one's condition mentally, and this was especially true in those days. And mentally, I was not ok. The scene replayed itself in my head for several weeks after, causing many sleepless nights and bouts of rage and panic.

I was told to rest, and I was back on patrol the following day. Robbo, though, had serious crush injuries to his legs and he too suffered in the years to come with PTSI that eventually saw him leave the Army.

The pilot who landed to collect Robbo had technically carried out an illegal landing but was quite rightly decorated by Her Majesty the Queen for his brave actions. As for me, I got stabbed in the back by my own Regimental Sergeant Major; a bully, and an ego-driven man who thought I was too young to be a sergeant and vocalised as much in the Mess on a regular basis.

I was made aware of his actions by friends who had witnessed them and warned me to watch my back. I approached my Company Commander and expressed a concern that the RSM was out to get me, to which he brusquely replied, "He is."

"Well, what are you gonna do about it"? I asked.

"Look, mate, truth is, if the RSM is out for you, there really isn't much I can do to stop it," he replied apologetically. Sincere or not, this did nothing to reassure me, and I found myself resenting him, the RSM and the whole situation, adding to my already deteriorating mental state. I'd essentially been told that called for a good ol' British stiff upper lip, and a pint of "suck it up, chief."

Some weeks later I was called by a member of our unit who was detached and teaching at the pre-deployment school. He informed me that our RSM had run a class there, where he told his recruits that I was the perfect example of someone getting their men injured because of an apparent failure to follow orders!

Now, those who know me are aware of how seriously I take the safety of my men and how important integrity is to me, and I was simply not going to let this pass.

I stormed over to the RSM's office. His fake, jovial welcome soon changed when I asked if he had said that, and I showed him my written orders from that day proving I did exactly what I was ordered to do, and highlighted that I only took one man with me as per the standard operational procedure that dictated that we to always be in pairs for security reasons.

He told me he couldn't remember what he said three days before and I called him a liar (full of shit, to be precise); not smart, but the truth, and indicative of my chronic habit of speaking my mind.

Needless to say, he yelled at me, I yelled back and walked away ignoring his demands that I return. A few weeks later he had his revenge when I was accused of something another Sgt was doing and, because I refused to name the Sgt, I was reduced in rank from Sgt back to Corporal and sent back to the covert unit.

It wasn't long after this incident that military explosives experts placed me and Robbo at less than 5ft from 10lbs of explosives at the point of detonation; saved by the fact the terrorists had placed it poorly and the primary blast blew in the opposite direction to us, that I started to rebel. We were caught in the side blast that buried Robbo and threw me into a cannon, headfirst, some 10 meters away. The blast, in addition to its physical effects, affected us both in other ways and while outwardly I dismissed it, looking back, my rise to the top took a major hiccup at that point; one that I never really truly recovered from.

I was back home in the covert unit with all the other rebels, and the best soldiers I have ever worked with; Hard, brave men who took more risks than anyone I ever knew. Our job was to get as close to terrorists as we could, and it was an exceedingly dangerous and stressful job.

On one operation, I and a very close friend, Terry - carrying only what we could get in our pockets along with 2 Browning Pistols and two HK53 SMGs - occupied what was left of the upper floor of a stable that IRA men were rebuilding during the day; we needed to know what they talked about.

Now, the upper floor was nothing more than a corner, the rest having collapsed, and so we were forced to squat or stand for the entire 48 hours we were up there, and if the terrorists had looked up at any stage, we would have been compromised and our back up; our Quick Reaction Force, was five  minutes away at best. That's an extremely long time to be fighting, outnumbered and stuck on the remains of an upper floor.

Thankfully, they were so completely oblivious to the possibility that two soldiers would do that, that they never looked up and we succeeded in our mission.

Sadly, the world lost Terry a few years ago to cancer, and it was a woefully sad day for me, as we had risked our lives together on several occasions. The tragedy of his passing was compounded by the loss of his younger brother, Darren, who was also stationed in our covert unit. Darren passed away a year later to a brain aneurysm. Words cannot describe how truly tragic and cruel it is to see how much these warriors survived on operations, only to have their lives taken by an illness at far too young an age. It just doesn't seem fair, these warriors had surely earned the right to live long, happy lives; another reason I am fighting to make sure an illness does not take more.

Out of the Fight?

S o, like millions of others, I left the military not only with lingering childhood issues but carrying the trauma associated with service. I had seen horrors, almost lost my life on several occasions and been subject to intense levels of stress, and nothing the Army did before I left was even remotely aimed at checking that or doing something to alleviate it. This was not done on purpose, but because the entire system is built on a foundation of "man the fuck up!"

The average soldier doesn't actually see full-on hand-to-hand fighting in his or her career, but every teeth arm soldier, soldiers like those in the Infantry and Special Forces, experience the true horrors of close-quarters combat as part of their day-job. For these soldiers, their sole purpose is to fight and serve for one or several operational deployments, where every day could possibly be the day they die. And even if it's not that day, if the soldier is narrowly able to avoid death, the stress of that day is etched on their soul.

The stress you went through sprinting out of the base gate, jumping from the hovering helicopter and waiting for the pain or the sound of a machine gun opening up on you; the inward gut-clench when you pass a bin or a parked car knowing that your enemy has a habit of putting bombs in them, means you suffer almost 24-hour stress that it's impossible to quantify to anyone who hasn't experienced it.

Whether you get shot at or not, the stress of placing yourself in harm's way is tremendous and the Army plays it down out of necessity; otherwise, they could never get you to go out the following day! I understand and agree with this, it is a way of working that is very much required, but when you are leaving, be that after three or 33 years, this down-playing of the danger and its effects on the psyche should stop, and proper care and attention must be made available.

For many, the only thing holding them together is their mates, and the fear of letting their mates down. So, when you find yourself alone and without your mates, the Darkness knows. It is waiting for it. It convinces you that your mates, brothers, friends, will think you weak, so you don't pick up the phone. It convinces you that these guys operated, or perhaps still operate, in the same system that you did but are apparently unaffected, so why would they be as empathetic or as understanding as you need them to be. And the truth is, sometimes they aren't, the mantra "man the fuck up" still rings true in their minds and reflect in their responses to your cries for help.

Thankfully, I personally am observing a major growth of awareness in veterans who are now reaching out, forming groups and bringing attention to the suffering of military veterans.

My hope is that no matter how successful my career is perceived by some, they see that I was still vulnerable and a victim of being recreated for a purpose and abandoned when that purpose was fulfilled.

My sincere wish for this book is to help save at least one life by showing that I am no hero or unbreakable soul. I am damaged, I am hurting inside every day, and every day I battle to reach the next day.

Some days are harder than others, some fly by without a care in the world. I have learned, though, and I would like to highlight, that the Darkness of PTS, depression, survivor's guilt, the grief of loss or just the recurring images of horrors you cannot erase often lurk at the back of your soul, concealed in the dark and waiting for a trigger; a life-changing moment or a moment of pain to slither back out and once again tempt you with lies of salvation and healing. The slow, almost fluid manner in which Darkness envelopes a soul, whispers soft lies and promises, turns people against those who would help with a false reality, until the Darkness seems, to all intents and purposes, as the only valid option.

You see a Darkness that seems to lead to salvation, light and an end to your pain; a path that feels like it's lifting your burden, that you can walk a little easier as though you have dropped your Bergen after a long tab (smoke). It offers a moment of calm and relief just before you apply the 3-4lb pressure it takes to send a bullet down the barrel, the calm before kicking the stool away or after swallowing the 50ᵗʰ tablet. A calm that robs you of life, of hope and of opportunity and a calm that rushes like a wave that can drown those you love that are left behind, unable to face life without you or are consumed by the guilt and their perceived failure, until they too start to hear voices from the Dark, and the self-created demons once again invade a soul.

I cannot speak for others, and I am by no means an expert. I merely wish to try and explain how I felt, how it consumed me and how I now recognise when I find myself in a dangerous place. I hope that it helps others.

I have frequently used the perspectives of a soldier and the military throughout this book because that is who I have been for most of my life, and where the majority of my life was spent or shaped. As such, this is a natural reference point for me. This Darkness, this mental illness that many still do not understand, can affect anyone. So please if you are not a soldier, please do not think I am not talking to you, because I am, and I wish to help anyone and everyone who finds themselves trapped in a dangerous downward spiral; no matter your background, sex, ethnicity or whatever your calling in life. You do not have to go to war to find trauma.

For me, the triggers have always been one of three things:

- Abandonment
- Shaming
- Not being/feeling good enough

When one of these triggers is pulled, and PTS is lurking, I find myself unable to stop saying and doing things that, deep inside, I know are hurtful, or just plain wrong, and for many years I didn't know why I continued to repeat this vicious circle.

Therapy has gifted me an understanding of the reasons behind my triggers and taught me the skills to determine my reactions now and not let this illness rule me.

For the truth is, it is an illness. Just because you cannot see or understand it, it is an illness and is incorrect in its labelling as a disorder. PTS is an illness because it can be cured, whereas a disorder is generic and an inherent part of the afflicted's makeup.

I believe that half of the issues relating to PTS are primarily due to a lack of understanding, and I am as guilty of this as anyone. I truly never researched PTS until it caused a rift between me and Liz. Even after Diane's death and I was diagnosed with chronic depression and PTS, I dismissed both out of hand and believed I was strong enough to deal with them on my own; a schoolboy error, but one created by how the Army designed my mindset.

"Can't means won't, and won't, means jail," was a common ethos in the Army, and because of this conditioning I was truly convinced I had everything in hand when anyone around me will tell you I definitely did not.

My illness blocked my ability to reason, and so there have been countless occasions where, in my head, my words and actions seemed right, appropriate and feasible. To the outside world, however, these words and actions were off the wall, aggressive, inappropriate or just plain nasty. I had limited patience, often blamed others for arguments that on reflection were entirely my fault and I was set on a path with as much conviction as I have ever had.

After Diane's death, my "Plan" was to follow her. I knew I had to make everyone think I was ok so that I would be left alone to plan and put everything in place. In my mind, I was a failure as a father and as a husband, and Diane's passing was all the proof I needed.

Everything I have recounted from that period comes from the small parts that I can actually remember, because grief has a habit of blocking memories to protect you, and there are many incidents that I have been told of that I still have absolutely no recollection of.

It was time to end it, go home and start over. I have always believed in reincarnation, so this seemed a perfectly logical plan to a brain devoid of the ability to think logically. The plan was not fool-proof, and the Darkness seemed impatient for me to end it and, to this end, would often trigger a downward spiral with a thought, act or situation that amplified my depression, causing me to forget the plan and reach for the gun.

One thing I do remember is the fact that even at those moments, I still worried about the aftermath. I didn't want my daughter to see it, as she was now in Phoenix with me. I worried about ruining the responding officer's life with the image I was about to make him or her suffer. I found a part of started me thinking and considering the implications of my planned suicide.

The spiral that was my path towards death developed branches, where at every turn there was a question to be answered or a fact to be considered. Solving these conundrums with apathy accelerated my descent so that I spun down the spiral at an ever-increasing speed.

The nagging questions persisted though, the answers became less obvious, the considerations greater. It was like something inside me was trying to prevent the rush to death, reminding me of my responsibilities, of the mental issues I was about to inflict on others. One of these questions always broke my mood, stopped the descent long enough for reason and doubt to apply the brakes and I would give it one more day.

Many of these occasions were at home, where I was alone and deep in the overwhelming thickness of silence that my home had become.

But one of the times that this happened has always stuck with me.

It was at a bar called the *Tilted Kilt*, a place Diane hated and would have lit me up for going into, largely because all the staff were young attractive females dressed in schoolgirl outfits, and a place I remember choosing to drown my sorrows to spite Diane for leaving me.

It was the first anniversary of her death, 8:47 p.m. on the 5ᵗʰ of August, 2010; one year to the second that she had passed. As the clock approached that time, I found myself slipping into a silent world, a world where I could see the bar, my friends, everything, but that felt like somebody was turning the volume down.

I found myself listening to memories being orated in my head. I was at the bar because Chris and another friend, Stephen, had realised the significance of the day and knew they needed to distract me as best they could.

But as the time approached, I found myself watching everyone else until they were busy, and slipping away, heading out of the side door to the car park.

Once outside, I walked to the wall at the rear of the car park and sat down, checked my watch and saw that I had four minutes to wait. Overwhelming thoughts of "This time last year I only had three minutes left" kept smashing around my head... two minutes left; I pulled my 1911 from my trouser waistband... one-minute left...

As I looked at the gun in my hand, I became aware of Stephen calling out to me as he walked towards me through the dark.

"What are you doing?" he asked, with a look that told me he knew full well what I was doing.

I sighed, "I just wanted to be alone mate, I'll be in soon."

"No, you won't, come on we are going now or I'm going to sit here with you while you do it."

The fall was broken, the spiral levelled as Stephen forced me to consider others, and the Darkness was cheated.

Most other spirals happened at home. Sat alone, in silence, and very much lost within my own head. On more than one occasion, I sat on my sofa at daybreak having just woken up with a cuppa and went over my life in my head.

On more than one occasion the day passed as a blur, and I remember asking myself why I couldn't see anything across the room, only to realise that it was dark outside again and I'd been sitting there in a blur, for 11 or 12 hours at a time.

At the time, I couldn't see the dangers of walking that far into your own inner self. But I now understand how people can reach that point of despair and isolation, where death seems a welcome relief, an almost natural next step.

I now see why many victims of suicide take themselves off to somewhere quiet, away from any chance of distraction from their purpose, and I don't believe they truly know what they are going to do until they find themselves deep inside their own mind, with only Darkness as a companion and with the desperate feeling that no other options remain. I know that for me, it felt that way. If I was busy, distracted, my thought process interrupted, the spiral stopped, and reason returned for long enough for me to decide on "another day."

I love my dogs; everyone knows that. For me, Mr. Oi and Miss Ey will forever have a special place in my heart. They both suffered immeasurably at Diane's loss, not just the fact that they had lost the only mother they had ever known, but also because I was in a mental condition that had me crying or angry all day. As my only companions, they often bore the brunt of my anger. But through it all, they never left my side.

I never actually ate a thing past two slices of toast for 32 days after Diane passed and survived on hot cups of tea and enough vodka to kill a small town, and so my poor dogs would often find Dad crashed out on the sofa, the floor, the sun-lounger or in bed, and they would climb next to me and box me in.

Miss Ey seemed to know nights were hard for me, as I was used to giving Diane a squish and I would often subconsciously reach out in the night looking for her. Miss Ey seemed to know, and as young as she was, only one year old, she spent every night pushed up against my back so I could feel someone there and get some rest. I have absolutely no doubts that she did that on purpose. I have no doubts that they sensed my moods and knew when I was in trouble.

I have lost count of the number of times during the first three years after Diane's death that I crashed mentally, often alcohol-induced and reached for my gun. Every time, without fail, Oi and Ey seemed to know and would come sprinting around the corner of the sofa and launch up into my lap. To my shame, on more than one occasion I pushed them off, shouted at them and attempted to continue down my intended path, only for them to jump back up and spread themselves out so they were hard to move.

Miss Ey had a look in her eye of such love and concern that it made me worry that the gunshot would frighten her, and I put the gun down. She wore that look her whole life and, when she became ill later in her life and vets told me to put her down, I refused, saying that for as long as she had that look of love for life and hope, I would never abandon her, just as she never did me.

The day just after her eleventh birthday, when I walked into the vets with Liz and they wheeled Miss Ey in on a stretcher, she could not even lift her head. My heart broke; the look was gone, and I knew she couldn't take anymore. I had to now let her go, the one female who had loved me through the worst moments of my life, without judgement or rejection. She looked across at Liz, who she adored, and she tried to lift her head. She passed with a paw in each of our hands.

I had lost Mr. Oi three years earlier when he was diagnosed with megaoesophagus, an illness that meant he could no longer swallow and had to be fed vertically to get food to his stomach. It was a death sentence, as pneumonia would eventually take him, and he passed two years later in his favourite place; the top step of my pool with his head on my hand. Miss Ey took that badly but never left my side. Now, at least, she is pain-free and back with her Mum and Brother.

———————◆

Now, many of you will not believe in life after death, in loved ones coming back to visit or clairvoyants, but I do; I have had too much happen for me not to. There are certain incidents in my life I cannot otherwise explain. This is one of them:

I had felt Diane's presence multiple times. In particular, I had, on many occasions, unexplainably walked through her perfume around the house and had no doubt she was letting me know she was ok and getting pissed off at me for trying to follow her.

Even in my depressed state, I had noticed the pups seemed to know everything I was thinking and decided that the solution was to shut them in the backyard and finally end it. So I coaxed them out, slammed the door quickly as they were both sharp enough to see a con quickly, and I walked around the house, making sure everything was in place; letters to certain people, passwords to stuff and a general organisational effort to hopefully ease the pain of those I would have left behind.

Once I was sure it was done, and, ignoring the barking and scratching to get in from Oi and Ey, I sat on my sofa, my back to the window so I could not see the pups, and picked up my gun. I remember going over all the details, some logical, some pretty random. It felt like a checklist.

I then checked the pistol was actually made ready. I didn't want my final act as a soldier to be an embarrassing click, and I put the gun in my mouth. I had laid out my dress blues and medals and a note asking to be buried as a soldier. I wanted to separate the medulla and achieve an instant death and so, by firing backwards through the mouth I knew the shock wave, let alone the bullet, would sever the brain stem and I would be gone.

Now, some of you are going to call bullshit on this, and I understand why, but on my current pups' lives, I swear this is what happened next.

As I increased pressure on the trigger, a cup - my empty teacup - that was on the side table next to me, launched itself across the room and shattered against the wall some 20ft away. Needless to say, it caught my attention and broke my mood! I remember throwing my gun down and shouting "Ok! Ok!" and having an image of an angry Diane in my mind's eye. I let the pups in, and they glued themselves to my lap for the next few hours.

Not long after this, a good friend and farrier to our horse called me and said, "Ok, this is gonna sound strange, but one of my clients is a clairvoyant and she told me today, completely out of the blue, 'you have a friend and I have a blonde woman bugging me to talk to him. can you ask him to call me?'"

I was sceptical, smelling bullshit, but I took her details and, with nothing better to do, I called. Prior to calling, I had removed all noise from the home and sat on our bed as the quietest place, to make sure she had nothing in the background she could pull cues from.

We spoke, and she explained her gift then and proceeded to tell me things she could not have possibly known. I know everyone says that, but in this case it's true. It's funny, but even though her voice did not sound anything like Diane's, her tone and delivery did, and it caught me completely by surprise. Sometime before her death, Di and I had decided to choose three questions to answer if we were the first to die, to show we were ok and prove it was us. Those answers were to the following unasked questions:

1. Were they ok?
2. What did Heaven look like?
3. Are there aliens?

The third, we assumed, would be far enough off base that no faker would guess it.

The first part of the conversation was about Di being angry at me. She said, "Drop the plan, you have something to do and cannot follow me. Stop trying to die!"

The fact that she said "plan," and that word had featured so centrally and prominently in my thoughts got my attention. As we progressed, she explained that the person she was talking with just showed images and she told me what she was seeing. She told me Di was showing her a classroom, like she was being debriefed and that told me she was ok. Question number one; answered.

Further into the conversation, she told me Di was, for some reason, now showing her an image of snow-capped mountains, green fields and a blue sky; like the scene from the sound of music... Heaven. Answer number two.

She then said Di had switched tone completely and was telling me she isn't always between Heaven and Earth. Sometimes they went to other planets to help other people…number three.

Now, many of you will say I grasped at what I wanted to hear, and to be honest I would have agreed with you if it wasn't for what happened next. She suddenly told me Di said to go and get her perfume. I was on our bed, less than five feet from her perfume and so, not to give any indication as to where I was in the house, I stood still in the bathroom for a few minutes before quietly sitting back on our bed. I told her I had it, and what she said next gave me chills.

She said, "Diane says you need to respray her pillow. Her perfume is fading, and she knows it helps you sleep at night, and she is worried that you are not sleeping."

Nobody knew I did that. I was worried people would think me stupid. At that point, I knew she was ok. That helped, but the battle inside of me was just beginning. Only this time, with her support, I would win.

Stopping the Spiral

Through my suffering, I have made the life-altering discovery that the downward spiral could be stopped simply by allowing reason, love or consideration back into your thought process, even for a few seconds. In those precious seconds, I found a reason NOT to end my life, and I grew from that. I drew strength from that, which enabled me to grow, stand back up, and find reasons to live.

As the days and months passed, the desire to end my life was forced further and further away, and while it still visits me every now and then, it has never won.

Sadly, however, eradicating the suicidal thoughts does not heal PTS or depression, and I continued on a self-destructive path that I have battled until this very day. I have recently read that if *you* don't address the issues of your childhood, your relationships will. Never have I read a phrase with a greater ring of truth.

Therapy should be a part of every business, a part of every walk of life, and a good friend of mine, Mike Iacobacci; a former Colonel from the 75th Ranger Regiment, suggested that everyone should see a therapist at least once every few months. He argues that it is good for the soul to vent and have an independent, trained individual to guide your actions and thoughts when needed, and I have to say I agree with him.

The ability to just vent to someone; someone who is trained to draw out hidden issues, is invaluable and I would strongly recommend it to anyone.

Speaking to a therapist does not mean you are a loony. It means you are normal, and that you need to get something off your chest.

We all bury stuff we should talk about because society has us believing the crap that marketing agencies put out to make sales without ever thinking of the mental issues they are causing; like beauty magazines that make perfectly normal girls feel like they have to starve themselves and look a certain way to be attractive, leading to bulimia and, at its worst, suicide.

Therapy saved my life and has helped make me a better person. I don't think I've ever been a bad person, but my inner phobias, my fears, held me back from ever having the courage to just be me. I wanted to fit in. I wanted people to admire and like me, and our world paints certain actions and images we feel we have to attain in order to be these things. I have a secret to tell you; it's total bollocks.

I was convinced I was inherently not good enough, and so I convinced myself that every girl I loved would eventually leave me. It was my own fears that pushed my relationships towards failure and not me ever not being good enough.

I was perpetually hypervigilant, looking for signs that were not there, putting intense pressure on partners in the process. I am certain that this played some part in my ex's cheating, but I feel her issues may have had more to do with it. That said, I don't believe her to be a bad person, just another soul in need of help. I hope she finds it, and finds herself in the process. I hope it leads to peace and happiness for her.

As time passed, I continually set new dates to complete my plan, pushing it further and further back as I found ever-increasing reasons to live. I was far from healed but now possessed a deep intuition, a feeling that there was something I was supposed to do, something that I had not yet done or achieved. One self-imposed delay was to wait for 2012 to see if the Mayans were correct. After all, if they were I would die anyway!

I had also found a book, which came as a result of watching a DVD with

Diane as it happens, but one that I never remembered until after she was gone, and I had a sudden overwhelming urge to read.

I remember a trip to Blockbusters one Friday, and after an hour we had the same dilemma that I know many couples have; neither of us could choose a film to watch. We were on the verge of leaving, heading toward the door when a movie caught my eye and I stopped and read the back cover.

Now, considering the title and synopsis of the story, it was most definitely a film that I wouldn't normally watch, and yet here I was, all but compelled to watch it, an urge that appeared to sit ingrained inside my conscience.

A few years later, the book upon which that film was based was to make a reappearance in my life. That book was called *Conversations with God*, written by Neil Walsh, and the mere fact many religions had called the book blasphemous and that several friends of mine told me to never mention that book in their house, compelled the rebel in me to buy and read the book.

This book changed my life. I certainly wouldn't say that it healed me, but what it did do was place me on a path of awareness; the awareness that I was not right and that I needed to try harder.

I think everyone should read this book with an open mind. The book centres on the author Neil and his life, telling the story of how his world crumbled around him and he found himself deep in a well of despair.

During a drunken pity-party in his own home, a home that he was about to lose, he challenged God out loud to explain to him why his life was falling apart. Why he had been singled out. The story then proceeds to explain how Neil was awoken later that night by a voice - God's voice - who proceeded to talk to Neil and have him write it all down so as to answer everyone's questions today; questions ranging from the moral and ethical, such as why and how could a God let children suffer, to the farcical; do aliens exist?

To organised religion, this man was a liar. To them, God simply could not have spoken to him. Now to me, they are happy to push the idea that God spoke to Moses, David and many others, so why not Neil?

Maybe God has seen enough to step in, and as he promised not to go ahead and drown us all again, he decided that this time he would talk and address questions.

I don't know the answers and I most likely never will, but it was enough to grab my attention and, considering that the book explains that organised religion has been corrupted by man, I can see the reason behind the church's resistance to this book.

For me, though, it all made perfect sense. For me, when used as a comparison, it also made the Bible much easier to understand and interpret, but in a different manner to the way prescribed by the church. It was an interpretation that I had felt already, for many years.

If this man is a fake, then in my opinion he is the best ever. The book simply resonates with logical answers to most of the questions that have been commonly asked by atheists, non-believers and people in general. It helps that it does it in a credible and believable way.

It is a struggle for many, but remember, we are so far on the King James Version of the Bible; a version where a monarch decided on what stayed and what was cut under direction from the church, to whom his power was dependent. This is one of many versions, versions that have been edited many times over since it was first translated into Greek for the popular consumption of Roman audiences.

It also points out that life is about you, your life, and not how much you do for everyone else. Donating to the church, for example, does not gain you eternal life in Heaven; it just makes Bishops rich.

It is by doing the right things in life that your soul grows, and you become truly closer to God, or The Universe, or whatever you wish to call it; but giving stuff to the church one minute and calling the Homeowner's Association on a neighbour the next is not saintly! One supposed good deed does buy immunity for a bad one.

The one idea I think I most struggle with is reincarnation, and the fact that Hell does not exist. Buddhists are way ahead in this regard, in many ways, and having an understanding of their beliefs is advisable, but all my readings have drawn me to the conclusion that all religions are simply alternate versions of the same events, and that doctrine has been changed by a select number individuals throughout history. Those who pull those strings have done so in the interest of personal gain, achieving this by reinventing the faith, renaming God and killing anyone who disagrees.

The fact that Hell does not exist and we do not go to purgatory, get judged and be punished drew a question from Neil that I also had myself; if there are no bad men and no Hell, are you saying that Hitler is in Heaven?

God's answer was that it's not that simple. The universe is far too complicated for Man to comprehend, but yes, when you pass, we are all eternal. Your life and actions are assessed.

He also points out that at the time, Hitler acted under the compulsion that he was doing good, and so he failed on that life lesson and was sent back as somebody else to try and learn that lesson again, in the correct way.

It makes sense when you view life as though it is a school. You choose your subjects, decide the experiences you wish to master in order to advance your soul, and off to Earth you go to learn. Free will is given to allow us to learn and not be led or guided. After all, if we are guided or pulled in a set direction, what lesson is learned? As we make mistakes, life gives us more chances until we pass.

Hence, we all find ourselves at times back in the same place as were some time before, presented with another chance to do the right thing. The entire concept is difficult to explain in short, so I would advise you to buy the version with all three volumes and read it for yourself. I read it three times before I could put it all in place, along with Bible studies at relevant sections, and for me, it answered my questions and made sense; to others, it is all lies and is a statement against the church. You decide.

For me, it is a go-to at times of doubt or struggle, and I have a system of opening it without looking and reading the first words my eyes fall upon. Each and every time, what has been there has been exactly what I needed to read.

Luck? coincidence? I have no idea, but if it helps me through and guides me, helps me to recentre my thoughts and control the triggers that ruin both my life and the lives of those I love, I'll take it.

On the day we buried my father, I took the dog for a walk before leaving for the funeral in the fields next to my parent's house to clear my head. This field has always suffered from flooding ever since I played in it as a kid, but I desperately needed the air. I was on the far side of the field, almost opposite my parents' house, when I found myself asking God the same question as Neil; Why?

I wasn't ready for anyone to answer, but I heard a voice, or an inner thought, or whatever you wish to call it, and I remember it just as clearly today as when I first heard it. In answer to my question why, the voice said,

"The world is a school and everybody has a lesson. When your lesson is learned, the school will close, and you will come home."

In that one sentence, I found peace and calm on one of the most difficult days in my life.

I have had multiple things happen in my life to make me want to give up, and I have tried to do just that on multiple occasions, but every time, something or someone intervened long enough to break my mood and allow a small amount of light to creep in.

There is always light in your life, but in such a confusing and painful place, sufferers often find themselves looking in the wrong direction and failing to find it. They see the look in a friend's eyes that says, "oh here we go again," or somebody says," "it's time you were over this," and you feel a burden. Your only recourse is to retreat into the Darkness, further away from the light. You tell yourself your mates are right and you are being a pain in the arse, so maybe it would be better if you were gone. This cycle repeats itself, and the more it happens, the closer to ending it you become.

We, as a society and as individuals need to learn more. We need to develop the understanding that a mental illness is nothing to be ashamed of; it's an illness. And like all illnesses, it can be treated.

As I mentioned at the very outset of this book, I fucking hate the term Post-Traumatic Stress Disorder. It is a term that conjures up images of somebody that is out of control, that is dangerous to others. Yet, statistics show that those most at risk from PTSD are the sufferers themselves, not those around them.

We owe it to them to learn more. We owe it to them to understand that, just because you cannot see the injury, or understand some of the things they do, the condition is real and it is debilitating, destructive, and, much too often, fatal.

We have a shocking 22 innocent people a day taking their lives, perhaps one of those is doing it right now, as you read about it. This has to stop.

And that number isn't even wholly indicative of the true picture. Those 22 are veterans. That doesn't include the many others who are not ex-service personnel; the civilians who take their lives. As I've already said, mental illness doesn't discriminate; it doesn't care if you have served or not.

Trauma can be a car accident, betrayal by a loved one, loss of your job, loss of a loved one, and much more. And please remember, one trauma is not worse than another. We should not tell someone to man up because we don't empathise with their experiences or feel ours are worse. Trauma is subjective, with differing levels of relevance and profoundness according to the individual.

Firefighters, police officers, doctors, nurses, and all manner of people fall victim to their own minds after witnessing a traumatic event and we need to truly understand that. Just because somebody isn't bleeding out of their ears, they can still be in pain.

Society has us more worried about what others think of us instead of learning to love and understand ourselves. We often portray an outward image that we think will make us popular, envied or desirable, and that image is very often not who we are or who we wish to be. Eventually, that fake reality will catch up with you.

We all do it, me included. But we have to get to a point where we realise that what other people think of us is nowhere near as important as what you think of you. The first step in standing back up for me was to see past the accusations, to see past my own feelings of self-doubt and to grow to like the person looking back at me in the mirror every morning.

Am I repaired now?

Not completely. And the truth is, I doubt I ever will be. What I am is better today than I was yesterday, and you can be damn sure that I will be better tomorrow than I am today. It's a process, not a one-time pill, and the rent on a fulfilled life is due daily, so it's a process of self-belief.

You have to find you, learn who you are and then take steps to become the real you, breaking down the walls you have built around yourself. Staying true to yourself and admitting your own weaknesses is a very hard thing to do, but it ultimately leads to a happier you. I was always told that truth sets you free, and for me, that has been true.

Am I ready to accept all my truths?

No, but I am willing to keep trying.

I have hurt people along the way. I am truly sorry for that. People have hurt me too, and now I try to see why people do what they do, look past their first intent, and try to find the pain inside that caused them to act in that way in the first place.

Forgiveness is the biggest gift we have, and to forgive is good for your soul; not just theirs. Harbouring hatred or anger just allows someone to live in your head, rent-free, and achieve nothing. They spoil your day and don't even know they are doing it.

So stop. Refocus, and only deal with the stuff you can change and ignore that which you cannot. Control your controllables. You can never turn off your emotions, nor should you; they combine to make you who you are, but you have to get to a point where your self-respect and integrity are stronger than your feelings.

That can be a difficult thing to do if suffering from PTSI, as the illness negates your ability to think outside of the emotional brain. But it can be done.

Meditation, breathing exercises, physical fitness and talking; these are all things you can do to help keep you level and focused when one of your triggers is hit. You will not, however, know what your triggers are if you do not seek help from a therapist, and so again I cannot recommend enough that you seek help to overcome your issues and self-doubt. The work of specialists, like Dr. Keerthy Sunder and his team, means that there is always hope. Reach out, ask for help. It does not make you weak.

I have been blessed with a life that from one side looks like a rags-to-riches story. A boy from a poor working-class home who is now friends with Royal Families and celebrities, but even a brief look behind the curtain shows quite a different story. Pain, depression, failure and self-doubt are present in everybody's life and mine is no different. At times it felt like I just could not get a break, but an inner belief that everything happens for a reason, and a desire to find the answers as to what that was, has always allowed me to get up, dust myself off and take another step into another day.

I have two main reasons for writing this book, both of which are related. Firstly, it does not matter where you grew up, what qualifications you have, the place you end up in life is going to be determined by you. You can either blame others for your circumstances, or you can make a plan, and follow it, pausing if you have to, but never quitting.

The second is; whatever life throws at you, NEVER QUIT, you either win or you learn and modify your plan as you need, and you take another step. Even the longest march starts with one step, and you can't see the end of a marathon when you start, so keep going. Ask for help, know your own limitations and value things in life that matter; people not possessions. Being honest with yourself is one of the hardest things you can ever do. We all make mistakes, we all hurt people we love, and we all have regrets. Life is too short to not act and put things right. As the saying goes, it does not matter how long you walk in the wrong direction, you can always turn around.

The year is 2022. I want to help end the tragedy of the 22 veteran suicides a day this year. I want to **End 22 in '22**. I ask everyone reading this to take time to look at themselves, ask hard questions and realise that you are never alone. There is always someone to call, text or visit and the Darkness lies. Even on the darkest nights, the sun comes up, and it's just a case of holding on until you are back in the light.

I said earlier in the book that suicide was not cowardly. It takes courage to pull that trigger, but it takes a very dark place for you to believe that there is no hope. There is always hope. Taking your life destroys so many other lives; the lives of those you most loved and those who most loved you.

One thing I did, and I challenge you to do, is I played the two songs below, sometimes on repeat, over and over until I put the gun down. They reminded me of the pain I would cause, of the pain Diane unintentionally condemned me to every day for the rest of my life. Your pain ends, but you create pain for those left behind.

So speak up, ask for help and tell someone that you are not ok. It's ok to not be ok! They do care, but you often present such a strong exterior that nobody can hear you cry out for help. Nobody can see how every minute is a battle. How could they? You are strong! You have just reached a point where you need people, not possessions. If you call loud enough, your friends will find you in the Dark.

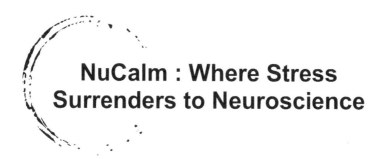

NuCalm : Where Stress Surrenders to Neuroscience

You may recall me discussing meditation and some mindfulness practices that I have adopted throughout my journey. Dr. Sunder has also discussed the importance and efficacy of mindfulness practices in treating PTSI at the very outset of this book. NuCalm has been a revelation within my own therapy, and I'd like to take moment to discuss how it works, and how I think it can help you.

I first became aware of NuCalm after a conversation with Dr. Sunder when we were in the early stages of the publication of this book. Dr. Sunder outlined the system to me, and his belief in it was clearly evident and enthusiastic enough to gain my attention. As a career soldier, my training has a tendency to make me sceptical of anything I cannot quickly grasp or see proven results on, but having spent many hours locked in the mental hell that is PTS, I wanted to learn more.

Dr. Sunder kindly invited me out to San Diego to attend his clinic and to try NuCalm for myself. I accepted his invitation, drove out and arrived with an open mind. Dr. Sunder's team were exceedingly professional and welcoming, taking the necessary time to explain, in intricate detail, the process I was going to be involved in and the various options on the program. In principle, the system involves a downloaded app, a headset, a light-blocking eye mask and a small, charged adhesive patch. This patch is electrically charged and is attached to your arm over the Pericardium 6 acupuncture point on your left wrist. You then don the mask and headset, get yourself comfortable and listen to the selected meditation program. As a beginner, they eased me into the two-hour program that is designed to relax, de-clutter and de-stress the brain.

I was taken aback by just how surprisingly peaceful and calming these two hours were for me. It was strange in the most pleasant of ways; I was personally aware that I was not asleep, but I never fully felt awake either, and at the end of the 2 hours I felt a sense of relaxation and clarity that had evaded me for years.

Now, my stress and PTS has made sleeping difficult for me over the last decade, and so I was surprised that, when I arrived back to my hotel room and lay on my bed fully clothed, I felt sleepy. Wanting to capitalise on this true rarity, I decided a quick nap was in order. The time was 7.15 p.m. I awoke, still fully clothed, at 06.30 a.m. the following morning feeling better in myself than I had felt in many years.

I have now been using NuCalm daily as a part of my regime for a little over a month at the time of writing, and I can honestly say I have never felt this alive inside, or as aware and driven as I do now, and I would unreservedly and without any hesitation recommend NuCalm to anyone. I now understand why the US Special Forces community, the US Air Force and many others now have adopted NuCalm as a part of their routine.

Mark Spicer
Sgt Major (Ret.)

The human brain is amazing and possesses capabilities beyond our comprehension. But it seems limited when it comes to intangibles. If we can't see it, touch it, smell it, or feel it, we have difficulty understanding it. This blind spot in our evolution allows the ruse of not accepting brain trauma as truth and perpetuates the problem for both the injured and the support system for the injured. Let's pierce the veil of apathy, ignorance, and confusion by explaining the facts.

The Physiology of the Human Stress Response

We shall begin by establishing a baseline understanding of the physiological changes that occur in the brain as a result of trauma. Humans have a central nervous system, a peripheral nervous system (motor and sensory nerves), and an autonomic nervous system. The central nervous system has one primary function above all others; to protect and keep us alive. Self-preservation is paramount and your central nervous system is always "turned on," evaluating your surroundings for safety and familiarity. Humans are creatures of habit, and our neuronal circuitry is designed to seek patterns and comfort in familiar surroundings. Your five senses and intuition collect and evaluate millions of data points daily, and even more when you are in new environments. When your central nervous system perceives a threat - real or perceived - it activates your "fight-or-flight" response through your autonomic nervous system.

The autonomic nervous system has two sides; the sympathetic nervous system (stress response) and the parasympathetic nervous system (rest and digest). The autonomic nervous system manages human stress, fear, anxiety, depression, and worry, in addition to the fight-or-flight response. In humanity's ancient past, the fight-or-flight response played an essential role in keeping our ancestors alive in the face of such dangers as predatory animals and natural occurrences, such as earthquakes, floods, and volcanic eruptions. Researchers have discovered that actual physical danger is not necessary to trigger the fight-or-flight response. It can also be triggered by your thoughts and beliefs. Simply put, if you habitually focus on thoughts and beliefs of a limiting or negative nature, you are causing your body to respond as if it is in danger. This results in the chronic production of stress hormones.

The communication pathway and mechanism that activates the fight-or-flight response is known as the hypothalamus-pituitary-adrenal (HPA) axis, which is a key part of the body's hormonal system. The purpose of the HPA axis is to spring into action at the first sign of any external threats that the body may face. When there aren't any threats, the HPA axis is in what might be described as "idle mode." This state of idleness allows the rest of your body to flourish the way that nature intended. But when the hypothalamus center in the brain perceives an outside threat, it signals the HPA axis to "roll out" and do its job, activating and mobilizing your mind and body to protect itself from danger. As soon as this signal is triggered, your body's adrenal glands increase their production of cortisol, adrenaline, and other stress hormones, releasing them into the bloodstream. Once this happens, the blood vessels that supply oxygen and nutrients to your body's cells and organs are constricted so that more blood can be made available to nourish the tissues of your body's major muscle groups, especially in your arms and legs, since it is primarily these extremities that the body uses to fend off external attacks and remove itself from harm's way.

Prior to this response, the blood in your body is concentrated in what are known as the abdominal visceral organs. These include your adrenal glands, kidneys, liver, gallbladder, stomach, intestines, colon, and appendix - the organs responsible for digestion and the absorption of foods and nutrients, excretion, and various other functions that allow for proper cell growth and the production of cellular energy. As blood is rushed to the tissues of the arms and legs, the visceral organs cannot function at 100%, causing all growth-related activities in the body to decline. As you can imagine, if this process continues for sustained periods of time, your body's overall functioning is compromised.

Chronically elevated stress hormones result in a chronically suppressed immune function, leading to a greater susceptibility to infectious disease. Additionally, because of how the visceral organs are also negatively impacted by chronic stress, many of your body's functions are also suppressed, setting the stage for impaired digestion, increased muscle tension, and the eventual decline in cell and tissue function, which can lead to a wide range of diseases, including cardiovascular disease and cancer. In addition, stress is also a major risk factor for gastrointestinal disorders, skin problems, neurological and emotional disorders, and a variety of conditions related to immune dysfunction, ranging from the common cold to arthritis, herpes, and even AIDS. Chronic stress in middle-age can also play a role in triggering the onset of Alzheimer's disease and dementia decades later, most likely because of the way chronic stress, through the effects of various hormones, can negatively impact the brain.

Sleep disorders are another area where stress is acutely involved. To achieve healthy sleep your body's normal cycle of hormone production must operate efficiently, especially regarding the release and management of cortisol. When we are healthy, cortisol levels are highest in the morning (6-8 a.m.) and lowest in the evening, where they continue to exist at a low level as we fall asleep. This allows your body to release sleep-enhancing hormones, such as melatonin and serotonin, which are vital to deep, restful sleep. Stress interferes with this process. When you are stressed, your cortisol levels remain high, even into the night, preventing restful sleep. Over time, the cycle of cortisol production becomes unbalanced, and in some cases even reversed, with levels spiking in the evening and falling in the morning, resulting in feelings of exhaustion. Insomnia and restless, fitful sleep (awakening throughout the night) are both common examples of sleep disorders that are associated with nighttime spikes in cortisol and other stress hormones, including, in some cases, adrenaline. Stress compromises the amount and quality of restorative sleep. This phase of sleep is the only opportunity your cells have to remove toxins and restore themselves. As you can imagine, a prolonged lack of restorative sleep decreases your cellular health and increases your susceptibility to disease.

Because of its impact on the brain and the body's nervous system, stress also plays a significant role in the onset of anxiety and depression. According to the National Institute of Mental Health, anxiety disorders are the most common type of mental illness in the U.S. It is also estimated that at least 10% of the U.S. population will suffer from serious depression at some point in their lives. In addition, it is common for people with an anxiety disorder to also suffer from depression or vice versa. Nearly 50% of all people in the U.S. diagnosed with depression are also afflicted with an anxiety disorder. Based on these statistics, it is not surprising that antidepressant and anti-anxiety medications are the leading class of drugs sold in the U.S. each year, accounting for over 270 million prescriptions for antidepressant medications alone (the entire population of the United States is approximately 330 million people). Given the steady increase of antidepressant drug use over the years, a growing number of health experts are warning that, as a nation, the U.S. is becoming addicted to such drugs, all of which are fraught with the risk for serious, even fatal, side effects.

Stress, more than anything else, has the greatest potential to sabotage every aspect of your life. Your health, your relationships, your work, your productivity, your brain function, cognitive abilities, and even your ability to simply enjoy your day can all be negatively impacted by stress. Yet, despite all that we know about the importance of managing stress, we, as a society, appear more stressed than ever before.

Post-Traumatic Stress (PTS)

The traumatized brain suffers restricted blood flow to key brain regions, including the prefrontal and frontal cortex (areas associated with our personality, our character, our executive function, our emotional intelligence, our analytical thinking, our patience, and our presence) and the hippocampus (our memory center). This restricted blood flow holds the trauma in constant focus for the brain - even during sleep - and results in an unhealthy sustained level of hypervigilance, impeding the body's natural processes for rest and recovery. In addition, when the brain experiences trauma, significant consequences occur beyond the physiological damage:

1. Your central nervous system loses faith in the universe and will fail to relax, feel safe, or feel comfortable in most environments

2. Your central nervous system loses faith in your ability to protect yourself from the universe.

These consequences are profound; your central nervous system is now constantly overreacting to threats, real or perceived, and is constantly activating the HPA axis by signaling the amygdala, which triggers your fight-or-flight response. This state of hypervigilance and the constant release of cortisol and adrenaline creates a toxic environment throughout the entire mind and body. Post-Traumatic Stress creates psychological, emotional, and physical fatigue due to a constant state of "high alert" and chronic stress. The traumatized brain MUST find a way to down-regulate the stress response to allow for healing to occur.

But how?

Meditation, yoga, Tai Chi, and deep breathing are all ways to self-regulate the stress response and get into balance, but what all of these approaches have in common is that they take time, effort, persistence, discipline, and patience, all of which are in short supply to a sufferer of Post-Traumatic Stress. What if there was an easier way, one that is proven to help?

That way is called NuCalm⸱; the world's first and only patented technology clinically proven to lower stress and improve sleep quality without drugs. NuCalm "switches off stress" and transitions you to deep relaxation and recovery within minutes, restoring your mind and body.

Introducing a Drug-Free, Patented, Clinically Proven Technology to Help

NuCalm was invented out of necessity by the brilliant quantum physicist, neuroscientist, and naturopath, Dr. Blake Holloway. Dr. Holloway served the veteran community in San Antonio, Texas for more than 40 years. His path to invention began in 1990, when he was determined to create a way to safely down-regulate the stress response without the use of drugs.

According to Dr. Holloway, "Following conventional therapies involving narcotic-based pharmaceuticals and cognitive behavioral therapy on a traumatized brain that is stuck in fear and hypervigilance is a death sentence for the wonderful people I love to serve. They won't take their life because they are cowards, they will take their life because they will reach a point of fatigue and a desire to stop living a life in a constant state of high alert."

NuCalm slows down brain wave function into alpha and theta zones (12Hz – 4Hz), so your mind and body restore and heal naturally. NuCalm scientifically sequences three components that closely and elegantly mimic your body's own physiological processes for managing stress and preparing for deep relaxation. With regular NuCalm use, you will regain control of your emotional and psychological well-being, where you will feel more present in the moment without judgment, more patient, and calmer, yet clear-headed and energized. In addition, you will enjoy the numerous and immediate health benefits that NuCalm provides. These include:

- Reducing stress and inhibiting the unnecessary production of stress hormones
- Calming nerves
- Improving sleep quality and helping to reverse sleep disorders such as insomnia
- Providing pain relief
- Relieving anxiety and fears
- Enhancing immune function
- Enhancing overall heart health and cardiovascular function
- Improving respiratory health and sinus conditions
- Restoring your body's natural biological clocks and circadian rhythms
- Accelerating recovery from physical exertion and injury

NuCalm is clinically proven to safely and rapidly induce parasympathetic nervous system dominance in PTS afflicted users which can dramatically improve sleep quality by down-regulating the sympathetic/adrenaline/cortisol response and suspending the brain in the natural recovery zone, which gets disturbed by combat, physical exertion, circadian rhythm disruption, and mental fatigue. NuCalm is the first demonstrated, clinically proven technology that uses biomechanically-oriented physics to naturally guide you to a place of peace and comfort. The physics embedded in the neuroacoustic software utilizes pitch and frequency matrices, binaural signal processing, and non-linear oscillating algorithms. According to research conducted by Dr. C.K. Peng at Harvard

Medical School, 20 minutes of NuCalm is equivalent to as much as 2 hours of restorative sleep.

NuCalm is safe, portable, and easy to use. It takes less than one minute to self-administer and within three minutes, you will experience parasympathetic nervous system dominance that results in the homeostasis of your autonomic nervous system in one treatment. NuCalm expedites recovery by oscillating your brain waves in the "healing zone" of theta brain wave dominance, including the hypnagogic, dissociative state of cellular restoration. This results in a synchronization of the heart and lungs to lower respiration rates to one breath every 10 seconds, maximizing oxygenation throughout brain and body, which removes lactic acid, lowers inflammation, and increases focus through oxygen-rich red blood cells in the frontal cortex and prefrontal cortex. In as little as 20 minutes of NuCalm, you will feel focused, energized, and able to perform at a high level without emotional distraction, fear, stress, or anxiety.

What People Have to Say About NuCalm

Renowned psychoneuroimmunologist, Janet Hranicky, MD, PhD, has been using NuCalm clinically for more than 8 years. Below you will find her clinical observations:

"NuCalm allows the old limbic area of the brain to experience a state of perceived safety and comfort, which triggers a parasympathetic response and the chemical changes physiologically connected with it. When the old brain is calm and feels safe, the frontal cortex can experience synchronicity and flow throughout the entire organism and allow the person to go into a state of deep relaxation. Perhaps, deeper than they might have gone for a long, long time. That state, we know, is a healing state. Going into and having periods of deep, restorative rest and relaxation is hugely important for getting better, getting well, and for creating optimal health and well-being. For most people who are suffering, there has been a chronic stress physiology involved in their life. The NuCalm state of deep relaxation allows for recuperation and a reboot of the system that can

provide the resiliency necessary to come back to where regeneration can occur. Regeneration occurs when we can bring down the stress physiology, because the immune system, the hormonal system, all of the healing mechanisms will begin to buoy back up and begin to self-regulate again."

- **Janet Hranicky, MD, PhD**

"Developing a beneficial meditation practice can take countless hours over a period of years. By using NuCalm I can effectively and quickly access a state of mind where I have the ability to respond instead of react. I use NuCalm because I have post-traumatic stress. With as little as 20 minutes a day I get to respond to my feelings and thoughts instead of reacting to them. When I have the ability to respond I can be humble, thoughtful, patient and kind. When I react instead of respond I can be aggressive, irritable, and fearful. NuCalm aids me into being the version of myself that is genuine and real. It is who I am without PTS."

- **Magnus Johnson, Former Green Beret Combat Veteran and President of Mission 22**

"In America, we are free because of the brave. And the reason the United States military special operations community is elite is because we have invested more into the operator's mind to ensure we are the most knowledgeable and best-prepared warriors on the battlefield. We must always maintain that edge and be able to tap into an even higher gear at a moment's notice. Operating in a constant state of alert has taken a toll on my mind and body and at 34 years old, beginning my civilian life, I struggle to down-regulate stress and I don't sleep well. In an effort to recover from my life in the military and regain my health, I've tried everything, from Alpha Stim, neurobiofeedback, and meditation, to apps such as Calm and Headspace. Nothing has made a positive impact on my stress and sleep until I began using NuCalm. I heard about NuCalm from a former special forces operator and to be honest, it sounded too good to be true. But I've been using NuCalm daily since January 2019 and it has changed my

life and brought me back to health. I am more calm, more focused, more patient, less reactive to situational stress and less agitated. I feel like myself again and my family has seen a big difference in my behavior at home. Raising 3 children and trying to assimilate to civilian life, NuCalm doesn't change the challenges I face, it changes how I interpret and respond to the challenges. I feel better, I sleep better, I'm more self-aware, and I'm more confident and optimistic about this next phase of my life."

- **Micah Robertson, Former Green Beret Combat Veteran**

"I've never been one to go and tell people how much I've endured during the course of 10 years as a special forces Green Beret and combat veteran... just knowing that they get to remain blissfully unaware of the evil that's out there means we were doing our jobs right. And the problems that came with the job were simply accepted as collateral damage in my mind... a necessity to ensure the mission was accomplished. Years of terrible sleep patterns, high-stress environments, and feeding off adrenaline put a toll on my body and mind. That's until I found NuCalm almost a year ago. I finally sleep through the night again and my body has recovered in ways I thought unimaginable. Now I won't rest until this product is in every operator's hands. They sacrifice enough ... I think we can take one thing off the list.... recovery for mind and body. In America, we are free because of the brave, and whatever we can do to help support our troops needs to be done. Thank you NuCalm."

- **Mike Squires, Former Green Beret Combat Veteran**

"As a 26-year veteran of the Special Operations community, and current program manager for the Human Performance Optimization (HPO) programs in my enterprise, I provide my highest endorsement for NuCalm as a technology and resource. NuCalm has unequivocally been one of the most effective stress mitigation, sleep improvement, and general wellness 'recovery modalities' we offer to our population. As an enhancing tool to our HPO programs, it has met

with resounding-positive feedback and almost immediate results. I am hard-pressed to identify any other device, gear, or similar system in this price range that offers the same. Jim Poole and his team of unparalleled experts have truly tapped into an amazing and effective application for the science of neuroacoustic software therapy, and beyond, through their work in this field and with NuCalm."

- **B.M. Lieutenant Colonel, Special Forces**

www.nucalm.com

Acknowledgements

This book has grown from an idea of one man trying to help a few by confessing his mistakes in life, to a global attempt to raise awareness of an illness that is being largely ignored. Now, I say illness, but in fact, it is an injury, an injury to the most amazing and mysterious part of the human being; the brain. I have always taught people that knowledge is the most valuable weapon we have, and knowledge is indeed power. With the help of an amazing team, we intend to educate the world on the fact that the brain, like any other part of the human, can be injured, and, like any other part of the human, it can be repaired. It is worth noting that a broken bone never fully heals back to the way it was before. It may be a little misshapen, it may ache from time to time, but it has grown back stronger than before, and injuries to the brain are the same. Just because we cannot see the injury, it does not mean it is not real. As humans, we believe in all manner of things we cannot see every day, with God being the most obvious for many people, or the invisible dark matter that holds the universe together like glue or even the oxygen that we take for granted every day. Each unseen, yet we have no doubts in our minds that they exist.

We know the brain exists. We know far more about it than most realise, but much of this fantastic biological computer remains unknown to us. We do know it can be injured, and Traumatic Brain Injury has become a well-established condition in the medical world. A lesser-known injury is that which is caused by Traumatic Stress, or PTSI. Thanks to the fantastic work of people like Dr. Keerthy Sunder and Jim Poole, we now know much, much more and have the means to repair the brain and help the injured recover. This book is dedicated to the work being carried out by men and women all over the world to help make PTSI and its associated treatments accepted and available to anyone who needs it and stop the needless suicides and destruction of life that it causes. This book, while based on my life, would never have been possible without an amazing team wrapped around me and deeply entrenched in its production, and I wish to thank them for all their hard work and dedication.

Firstly, to my very good friend and brother Michael Giuliano, who introduced me to the amazing woman and unstoppable force that is Stephanie Pierucci. Stephanie was the first to see the potential of this story, and when it almost died at birth due to the lack of funds to move it forward, she showed the draft to Dr. Keerthy Sunder, who then took it upon himself to fund the project; an act of kindness that will no doubt save thousands across the world as this project educates and leads people out of the Dark. Stephanie built a team around her of like-minded go-getters, and it started to gather momentum.

Next, thank you to Julie Husch, who suffered my twisted sense of humour daily with grace and tact; Luis, Garima, Shaun, Corey and Dale for their help in shaping my story; Dr. Jothsna, who, with Dr. Keerthy Sunder, put me through my first NuCalm sessions and of course Jim Poole, whose NuCalm treatment, I believe, will help change the world.   Finally, I want to thank all those who have been there for me during my battle. There are too many to mention, but certain people cannot be ignored in what they have done for me: My Mum; Steve and Gemma, my amazingly tolerant kids; my cousin Jo; Liz; my brother Dean; Tony and John; Tom; Brian K; Mike I, and without doubt, my seven-fur missile German Shepherds: Mr. Noi, Miss Boo, Mr. Kai and Miss Ziva, Nala, Liat and Gwen, angels without wings and proof that Dog is God spelt backwards.

Thank you all, together we are STRONGER.

S|T|R|O|N|G|E|R

Now that you have had the chance to connect with my battle and victory over PTSD, head to www.OutdanceTheDevil.com to grab your STRONGER poster for free.

Alone you are strong, together we are STRONGER!

Stay in the Fight
Tell Others You Need Help
Resist the Dark
Own It
Never Quit
Grow From the Pain
Elevate Self Belief
Resist Repeats

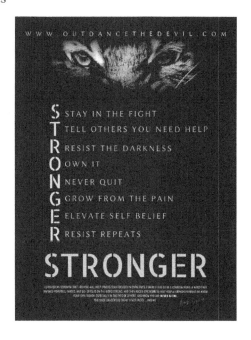

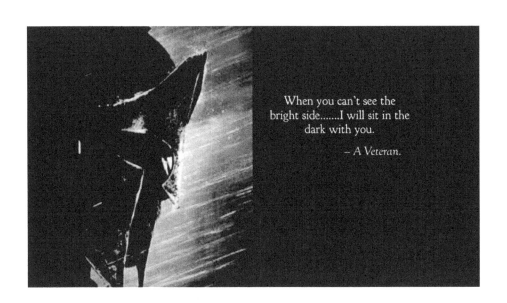

When you can't see the bright side.......I will sit in the dark with you.

– A Veteran.

Epilogue

Dear Soldiers,

Maybe you're a wife and mom who's stayed in an abusive marriage for the sake of the kids.

Maybe you're a lover who's been cheated on or, worse yet, abandoned by your lover.

Maybe you're an adult child who's suffered emotional, physical or sexual abuse.

Maybe you're a refugee from a war-torn country.

All of us who've escaped these circumstances and hold this playbook to healing are soldiers.

Thank you for joining me on this journey. My only prayer is that together we can end the number of men and women suffering in the darkness from PTSD every day. Now consider: what would a world look like for your parents, your children, your best friend, or your peers if they were the beneficiaries of this book?

Help me create that world.

Here's how you can support your own recovery from PTSD and share **Outdance The Devil** with people you love.

1. Write an amazing five-star review wherever you purchased this book and/or wherever you love buying books. A list of places where it's available can be found at **www.outdancethedevil.com.**

2. Ask your local bookstore to stock **Outdance The Devil**. This helps us get more inspiration and positive change into your local community.
3. Run an **Outdance The Devil** support group with peers. Challenge one another to read several chapters per week. Offer a shoulder to cry on or a high five as others process my trauma as well as their own. Make this space safe and sacred to share with one another... ideally not in a coffee shop unless it's after hours!
4. Learn more about Mark Spicer and how to plug into his community by visiting **www.OutdanceTheDevil.com**
5. Sport your End 22, and STRONG Merchandise by visiting **www.OutdanceTheDevil.com** where you'll find hats, tees, tanks, hoodies, poker chips, STRONG Posters, wristbands, and mugs.
6. Keep yourself accountable to your own recovery by printing your STRONG Poster as a FREE PDF Download from **www.outdancethedevil.com** or by purchasing your high-quality color copy in our Merchandise Store and hang it proudly in your office, on your refrigerator, on your bathroom mirror, and anywhere else you need that gentle reminder that **you are STRONG.**
7. Purchase a copy of **Outdance The Devil** for everybody you love at your favourite online bookstore.

8. And most importantly, begin your Mindfulness work with our app found at **www.outdancethedevil.com**. Put the app on your cell phone home screen and take just 15-20 minutes daily to sit in silence and reflect on your strength and the battles you've yet to fight... and win.

You've got this, mate.
Stronger Together,

Mark Spicer

Mark Spicer

Appendix
Dr. Keerthy on Nervous System Regulation

"I could not believe what happened when I began meditating. It was the difference between heaven and hell. It was absolutely transformational."
Vietnam Marine Veteran Dan Burks

Retired Platoon Sergeant Leshonda "Shy" Gill, who served in Iraq, shares how mindfulness saved her life. She says, "I know the trauma that got me onto that window ledge, but I also know what got me out of that window ledge and why I'm here now— meditation. To know that as small of a concept as 20 minutes can make me feel like I feel now—that's a gift that you can't buy."

Meditation will see you through tough times and many life changes, keeping you sane, grounded and real. Life is challenging enough; you never know what will arise next and only when your mind is clear and focused can you make the best decisions and transform yourself into the person you want to be.
I am proud to partner with Mark Spicer on his courageous book, "Outdance The Devil: A Soldier's Account of the Scariest Enemy He Ever Fought."

During the past several decades as a surgeon, psychiatrist, and medical doctor specialising in treating Post-Traumatic Stress, I've learned that Mindfulness is the ultimate key to resilience for those of us surviving with Post-Traumatic Stress. And happily, mindfulness is a universal practice enjoyed by billions of people around the world that has been documented for 3,000 years of human experience. What's more, the practice is free, and you can start right away.

I began publishing articles about Mindfulness while working with the Alcohol and Drug Treatment Program with the San Diego Veterans Administration (VA)

Health Care System in San Diego, CA, USA. I learned that resilience is the capacity to withstand stress and catastrophe. Psychologists and philosophers have long recognized the innate capabilities of humans to adapt and overcome risk and adversity.

Being resilient does not mean passing through life without experiencing stress and distress. Humans naturally experience grief, sadness, and a range of other emotions concerning adversity and loss. However, when the right social support structures are in place, individuals and communities are able to rebuild their lives, even overcoming devastating events, including Addiction and Post-Traumatic Stress.

The characteristics of resiliency include intellectual mastery and curiosity, compassion with detachment, and the ability to conceptualise and attain the conviction of one's own right to survive[1]. Further, an ability to imagine, remember and invoke positive images, as well as having a goal to strive toward, are also identified as resiliency characteristics.

Other such characteristics include attracting and utilising appropriate support, creating a vision to restore moral order, possessing the ability and willingness to assist others, having a sense of true self and developing a heart-centred fighting spirit[2].

Mindfulness is usually regarded as involving two concepts: awareness of and attention to the present moment and acceptance without judgement. Creating an awareness of the present moment means that an individual observes his or her feelings, thoughts, and sensations and directs these to the current moment. Attending to a current moment requires adopting a stance of willingness and acceptance so that one can experience emotions and thoughts without judgement[3].

1   Lutha SS, Cicchetti D (2000) The construct of resilience: implications for interventions and social policies. Dev Psychopathol 12: 857-885.

2   Apfel RJ, Simon B (1996) Minefields in their hearts: The mental health of children in war and communal violence, Yale University Press, New Haven, USA.

3   Meditation and Mindfulness - Counseling Center (NDSU) (2009).

While, on the whole, humans are capable of exhibiting great resilience to adversity, exposure to the ravages of war places soldiers in a particularly high-risk category for developing an addiction or PTSD. Recent statistics on the Iraq and Afghanistan wars show that PTSD and other mental health issues pose some of the most significant health challenges for veterans. Currently, the prevalence of PTSD among Iraq War veterans is estimated to be as high as 20%[4].

However, since symptoms often take months or years to appear, that figure is expected to rise, and future projections place the rate of PTSD in this group of veterans in the range of 35%[5]. This would closely correlate with, and potentially surpass, the 30.9% lifetime prevalence of PTSD among male Vietnam War veterans. Untreated, PTSD leads to tragic and costly consequences, including addiction. Army suicide rates reached a 30-year high in 2008, having more than doubled since 2001[6].

This trend, which has been claiming more lives than those lost in combat, is expected to continue into the foreseeable future. Among Vietnam veterans with PTSD, 34.2% have been arrested or jailed at least once and 11.5% have been convicted of a felony[7]. PTSD has also been found to impair cognitive function. Substance abuse and addiction are rampant among veterans with PTSD, with lifetime alcohol abuse among male Vietnam veterans running at 39.2%[8]. The two

---

4   Wolf EJ, Mitchell KS, Sadeh N, Hein C, Fuhrman I, et al. (2015) The Dissociative Subtype of PTSD Scale: Initial Evaluation in a National Sample of Trauma-Exposed Veterans.

5   Wolf EJ, Mitchell KS, Sadeh N, Hein C, Fuhrman I, et al. (2015) The Dissociative Subtype of PTSD Scale: Initial Evaluation in a National Sample of Trauma-Exposed Veterans.

6   Schry AR, Rissling MB, Gentes EL, Beckham JC, Kudler HS, et al. (2015) The Relationship Between Posttraumatic Stress Symptoms and Physical Health in a Survey of U.S. Veterans of the Iraq and Afghanistan Era. Psychosomatics 56: 674-684.

7   Schry AR, Rissling MB, Gentes EL, Beckham JC, Kudler HS, et al. (2015) The Relationship Between Posttraumatic Stress Symptoms and Physical Health in a Survey of U.S. Veterans of the Iraq and Afghanistan Era. Psychosomatics 56: 674-684.

8   Wolf EJ, Mitchell KS, Sadeh N, Hein C, Fuhrman I, et al. (2015) The Dissociative Subtype of PTSD Scale: Initial Evaluation in a National Sample of Trauma-Exposed Veterans.

conditions occurring simultaneously confound clinicians' efforts to effectively treat either one[9]. These illustrate just a few of the long and growing list of physical and mental health effects of PTSD, including addiction; all of which urgently require more accurate identification as well as more effective treatment approaches in order to bring much-needed hope and healing to veterans with PTSD. The purpose of the listed published paper was to conduct a qualitative research review on how mindfulness has been used as a way to help veterans with PTSD or addiction to build resilience. (Sunder, J Addict Res Ther 2015, 6:4)

Resilience and Mindfulness

The practice of mindfulness is rooted in reflective traditions that seek increased awareness through meditation. The main aim of mindfulness is to cultivate an attitude of compassion and curiosity to the present moment.

Recent years have seen more Western mental health treatment programs and researchers including mindfulness in their treatment proposals. How does a culture of mindfulness create resilience in military veterans, particularly given the increasing numbers of veterans presenting to the VHA seeking treatment for post-traumatic stress disorder? Proponents have suggested that mental training, especially through meditation and similar practices that encourage the individual to safely explore his or her inner life, produces significant changes in emotion and cognition.

Mindfulness involves a wilful and purposeful approach to regulating one's attention, either for purposes of self-exploration and relaxation or transcendence and personal growth. This concept appears in the form of meditation and consists of two categories: physical body movement and mindfulness meditation.

The first category includes movement disciplines, such as Yoga, Tai Chi, or Qigong. The second category involves mindfulness meditation, mantra

---

9   Schry AR, Rissling MB, Gentes EL, Beckham JC, Kudler HS, et al. (2015) The Relationship Between Posttraumatic Stress Symptoms and Physical Health in a Survey of U.S. Veterans of the Iraq and Afghanistan Era. Psychosomatics 56: 674-684.

meditation, or body scan meditation[10]. While these mindfulness practices appear mechanistically distinct, their effects often overlap so that they achieve similar effects.

Maintaining focused attention on an object or physiological variable requires the ability to suppress the attention of outside influences. When applying these techniques, the meditator adopts an attitude of focused concentration and attention. This concept is thus referred to as mindfulness or mindful awareness. These actions elicit a physiological relaxation response that acts antagonistically to the stress response.

Many of the physiological effects of mindfulness are clinically measurable and have been found to offer therapeutic benefits that help build resilience for patients with PTSD and resolve addictive behaviours for patients with substance abuse or addictions, especially in areas such as brain function[11] and immune system function, attention and memory, self and auto-regulation (including control of stress and emotions, anxiety, and depression[12]).

Western and Buddhist scholars concur on the value of meditation for managing symptoms of PTSD and substance abuse. The Dalai Lama, the head of the Tibetan spiritual movement of Buddhists, agrees that the unity of all things begins in the mind.

Tibetan monks have a particular interest in the workings of the human brain. They spend several hours a day in meditation and claim that this activity increases brain functionality, concentration, and learning ability, especially with regard to memory.

---

10   Schmidt S, Walach H (2014) The neurobiology of meditation and mindfulness. Meditation--neuroscientific approaches and philosophical implications. Springer International Publishing.

11   Davidson RJ, Kabat-Zinn J, Schumacher J, Rosenkranz M, Muller D, et al. (2003) Alterations in brain and immune function produced by mindfulness meditation. Psychosom Med 65: 564-570.

12   Schmidt S, Walach H (2014) The neurobiology of meditation and mindfulness. Meditation--neuroscientific approaches and philosophical implications. Springer International Publishing.

In "Training the Brain" we see the scientifically proven facts that mindfulness, in the form of meditation, plays a critical role in improving the performance of the brain and, in fact, can alter brain structure. The brain can be trained and modified in specific ways that bring about lifestyle changes and behaviour modifications that considerably reduce post-traumatic stress[13]. To Tibetan monks, meditation is simply a way of everyday life. It is a regular exercise to control the brain and experience relaxation. However, scientific evidence shows that non-Buddhist patients with PTSD and addiction who use these techniques can also improve their brain performance and increase the amount of grey matter in their brains.

Contemporary Evidence for Mindfulness in PTSD and Addiction

Research suggests that when veterans with PTSD receive even a short introduction to mindfulness through meditation, they may experience huge leaps in symptom resolution[14]. Underlying variations with regard to different aspects of mindfulness may make certain individuals more predisposed to developing PTSD. In a study that compared mindfulness in veterans with and without PTSD, those with PTSD consistently scored lower on tests for mindful non-judging.

However, the two groups scored equally on a mindful awareness scale, leading researchers to postulate that the two aspects of mindfulness occur in different brain areas, with mindful non-judging being a function of the medial prefrontal cortex, which inhibits the amygdala, while mindful awareness is mediated through an unrelated neural network.

Moreover, for a patient with PTSD, symptom resolution may rely more on the attitude associated with a memory than simply possessing mindful awareness of the memory[15]. In a Research study, statistically significant self-reported decreases in symptoms and improvements in quality of life in veterans with

---

13   Rabipour S, Raz A (2012) Training the brain: fact and fad in cognitive and behavioral remediation. Brain Cogn 79: 159-179.

14   Shore A (2004) Advances in Neuropsychoanalysis, Attachment Theory, and Trauma Research: Implications for Self Psychology. Psychoanalytic Inquiry: 22.

15   Wahbeh H, Lu M, Oken B (2011) Mindful awareness and non-judging in relation to posttraumatic stress disorder symptoms. Mindfulness (N Y) 2:219-227.

PTSD was noted within 8 twice-weekly treatment sessions[16]. A mindfulness-based cognitive therapy (MBCT) program adapted for patients with combat-related PTSD found clinically meaningful decreases in PTSD symptom severity. Particular areas of improvement included avoidance/numbing symptoms and a tendency to self-blame.

All participants had suffered from long-term PTSD (for more than 10 years) with the majority experiencing symptoms for more than 30 years. Additionally, many had previously gone through extensive psychiatric and pharmaceutical treatments[17].

A mindfulness-based stress reduction program that focused on fostering self-compassion was effective at regulating mood in veterans with PTSD who have difficulties with mood and emotion. The treatment improved overall mood and reduced negative ideation, dysfunctional attitudes, depression, and anxiety.

Physiological symptoms including dizziness, depression, fatigue, and tension were also reduced due to autonomic regulation effects of the practice. Researchers recommend the technique as being highly effective and cost-saving, even when used for brief periods[18].

Female veterans with PTSD report greatly reduced recovery time from dissociative episodes following participation in a treatment protocol that combines massage, mindfulness, and psychotherapy. The treatment has also been found to bring repressed emotions into conscious awareness, allowing them to be processed during psychotherapy[19].

16   Azad Marzabadi E, Hashemi Zadeh SM (2014) The Effectiveness of Mindfulness Training in Improving the Quality of Life of the War Victims with Post Traumatic Stress Disorder (PTSD). Iran J Psychiatry 9: 228-236.

17   King AP, Erickson TM, Giardino ND, Favorite T, Rauch SA, et al. (2013) A pilot study of group mindfulness-based cognitive therapy (MBCT) for combat veterans with posttraumatic stress disorder (PTSD). Depress Anxiety 30: 638-645.

18   Hoffart A, Øktedalen T, Langkaas TF (2015) Self-compassion influences PTSD symptoms in the process of change in trauma-focused cognitive- behavioral therapies: a study of within-person processes. Frontiers in Psychology 6: 1273.

19   Price CJ, McBride B, Hyerle L, Kivlahan DR (2007) Mindful awareness in body-oriented therapy for female veterans with post-traumatic stress disorder taking prescription analgesics for chronic pain: A feasibility study. Alternative Therapies in Health and Medicine 13: 32–40.

PTSD that occurs concurrently with substance addiction is highly prevalent and poses particular treatment challenges. According to the U.S. Department of Veterans Affairs, in the general population, 46.4% of individuals with lifetime PTSD also meet the criteria for substance abuse disorder. Though comparable epidemiological studies have not been conducted among veterans, the 1980 National Vietnam Veterans Readjustment Study found comorbid substance abuse disorder in 74% of Vietnam veterans with PTSD. Mindfulness training is yielding promising results for this group. In a recent study of veterans with comorbid PTSD[20] and alcohol use disorder, an 8-week mindfulness-based stress reduction program resulted in significant symptom reduction, with benefit retention in areas including depression, behavioural activation, acceptance, and mindfulness at 6 month-follow-up[21].

Preliminary evidence shows that prescription opioid misuse among chronic pain patients may be managed or prevented through mindfulness training. Compared with support group therapy, a mindfulness-oriented recovery program resulted in significant reductions in pain severity and pain-related functional interference at a 3-month follow-up[22].

Patients undergoing methadone maintenance treatment for opiate addiction received 8 group sessions of mindfulness training that involved focusing on present-moment changes in their thoughts and physical sensations and welcoming new thought patterns without expending effort to change or challenge

20   Hamblen JL, Kivlahan D (2015) PTSD and Substance Use Disorders in Veterans - PTSD: National Center for PTSD.

21   Ralevski E, Olivera-Figueroa LA, Petrakis I (2014) PTSD and comorbid AUD: a review of pharmacological and alternative treatment options. Subst Abuse Rehabil 5: 25-36.

22   Garland EL, Manusov EG, Froeliger B, Kelly A, Williams JM, et al. (2014) Mindfulness-Oriented Recovery Enhancement for Chronic Pain and Prescription Opioid Misuse: Results from an Early Stage Randomized Controlled Trial. Journal of Consulting and Clinical Psychology 82: 448– 459.

old patterns. Post-therapy survey revealed higher scores on mental, emotional, physical, and social quality-of-life scales compared to controls[23].

Risk of substance abuse relapse remains a prevalent problem following standard 12-step and psychoeducational treatment programs. Mindfulness combined with cognitive-behavioural relapse prevention has been shown to provide superior benefits compared to conventional treatments. In one study, participants reported significantly fewer days of substance use and heavy drinking at 6- month and 12-month follow-up compared to a group that received treatment as usual[24].

Participants in one study of a mindfulness-oriented recovery enhancement program reported significantly improved general activity levels, mood, walking ability, relationships, sleep, and overall enjoyment of life compared to support group-based therapy, with psychological, though not physiological improvements persisting at a 3-month follow-up[25].

Neuroscience of PTSD and Addiction

Scientific evidence proves that a considerable increase in activity of the lei-anterior brain is directly proportional to positive feelings, and this improves the functionality of the immune system[26]. Davidson, et al. used this assumption in investigating significant activation of this part of the brain and its association

23   Hosseinzadeh Asl NR, Hosseinalipour F (2014) Effectiveness of Mindfulness-Based Stress Reduction Intervention for Health-Related Quality of Life in Drug-Dependent Males. Iranian Red Crescent Medical Journal 16: e12608.

24   Bowen S, Witkiewitz K, Clifasefi SL, Grow J, Chawla N, et al. (2014). Relative Efficacy of Mindfulness-Based Relapse Prevention, Standard Relapse Prevention, and Treatment as Usual for Substance Use Disorders: A Randomized Clinical Trial. JAMA Psychiatry 71: 547–556.

25   Garland EL, Homas E, Howard MO (2014) Mindfulness-Oriented Recovery Enhancement Ameliorates the Impact of Pain on Self-Reported Psychological and Physical Function Among Opioid-Using Chronic Pain Patients. Journal of Pain and Symptom Management, 48: 1091–1099.

26   Kabat-Zinn J, Massion AO, Kristeller J, Peterson LG, Fletcher KE, et al. (1992) Effectiveness of a meditation-based stress reduction program in the treatment of anxiety disorders. Am J Psychiatry 149: 936-943.

with antibody titers after a shot of flu vaccine to participants completing a mindfulness course and those on the waiting list.

The nature of increase in cortical activity had a directly proportional relationship with an increase in antibody titer. The mind and the body cannot be easily separated as shown in this experiment. The central and the peripheral processes have an interlinked functionality and the activity of one part affects the other[27]. Different types of meditation result in differences in brain activity.

In an experiment by Lutzet al., robust long-distance phase-synchrony and gamma-band oscillation was recorded during generation of non-referential states of meditation. This research focused on the compassion state of meditation, though it is evidently clear that other forms of meditation would yield similar results. Essentially, this experiment corroborates and supports the thesis of this review article. First, it answers that mindfulness is essential in affecting brain structural functionality and secondly, brain functionality is essential in studying resilience[28].

Contemporary Research has also demonstrated that our core sense of identity is deeply connected to our body identity. An area of the Brain called the "Insula" interprets body sensations and brings them into conscious awareness. Damasio et. al. have demonstrated decreased activation of the Insula and other areas related to self-awareness in persons who have experienced trauma[29].

Modern imaging techniques have provided a wealth of insight into the neurobiology of addiction. SPECT studies have found decreased serotonin activity via reduced SERT (Serotonin Transporter) availability in brainstems of alcoholics but similar SERT availability between heroin users and health

---

27   Davidson RJ, Kabat-Zinn J, Schumacher J, Rosenkranz M, Muller D, et al. (2003) Alterations in brain and immune function produced by mindfulness meditation. Psychosom Med 65: 564-570.

28   Lutz A, Greischar LL, Rawlings NB, Ricard M, Davidson RJ (2004) Long- term meditators self-induce high-amplitude gamma synchrony during mental practice. Proc Natl Acad Sci U S A 101: 16369-16373.

29   Vianna EP, Naqvi N, Bechara A, Tranel D (2009) Does vivid emotional imagery depend on body signals? Int J Psychophysiol 72: 46-50.

controls. However, higher levels of SERT availability has been associated with an increased likelihood of relapse, indicating potentially conflicting roles of serotonin in addiction[30].

PET studies have revealed reduced dopamine receptor expression in the striatum of drug addicts. Whether this represents a predisposing factor or compensatory reaction to chronic stimulant drug use is unknown at this time. Through 20 years of PET studies in the realm of addiction, a consensus has emerged that addiction generally results from a combination of pre-existing individual neurochemical risk factors, environment, and drug exposure[31].

PET scans of cocaine users have shown that when severely addicted individuals view videos of cocaine use, a significant release of dopamine is observed in the dorsal striatum, leading to drug cravings. EEG scans confirm increased cortical activation in response to drug cue exposure in both alcohol and cocaine-addicted individuals[32].

PET imaging has demonstrated that chronic smoking reversibly up-regulates the number of acetylcholine receptors in the brain. The amount of tobacco consumed by the average daily smoker results in nearly complete occupancy of one of the brain's most common acetylcholine receptors and which is responsible for nicotine-induced tolerance and sensitization[33]. Cigarette smoking also influences the brain's reward circuitry by stimulating dopamine release in the ventral striatum[34].

---

30   Lin SH, Lee LT, Yang YK (2014) Serotonin and mental disorders: a concise review on molecular neuroimaging evidence. Clin Psychopharmacol Neurosci 12: 196-202.

31   Cumming P, Caprioli D, Dalley JW (2011) What have positron emission tomography and 'Zippy' told us about the neuropharmacology of drug addiction? Br J Pharmacol 163: 1586-1604.

32   Parvaz MA, Alia-Klein N, Woicik PA, Volkow ND, Goldstein RZ (2011) Neuroimaging for drug addiction and related behaviors. Rev Neurosci 22: 609-624.

33   Parvaz MA, Alia-Klein N, Woicik PA, Volkow ND, Goldstein RZ (2011) Neuroimaging for drug addiction and related behaviors. Rev Neurosci 22: 609-624.

34   Parvaz MA, Alia-Klein N, Woicik PA, Volkow ND, Goldstein RZ (2011) Neuroimaging for drug addiction and related behaviors. Rev Neurosci 22: 609-624.

In cocaine-addicted individuals, SPECT imaging shows decreased regional cerebral blood flow in the lei and right caudolateral orbitofrontal cortex, bilateral superior temporal gyri and lei middle temporal gyrus. It is thought that the orbitofrontal cortex exerts inhibitory control over ongoing behaviour, indicating its potential contribution to the inability of cocaine-addicted individuals to predict the consequences of their actions, therefore hindering their ability to self-regulate behaviour[35].

MRI studies have revealed dysregulation in brain areas responsible for reward processing and cognitive control, notably the mesolimbic prefrontal pathway, in heroin users. Specifically, an inverse relationship is seen between sensation-seeking behaviours and midbrain size[36] significantly lower white matter is often present in the corpus callosum, fornix, external capsule, superior longitudinal fasciculus, and cingulate gyrus of individuals with alcohol use disorders, as evidenced by fMRI.

This imaging technique has also led to the discovery of a gender difference in alcohol effects on the brain whereby higher drinking frequency leads to greater neurotoxicity and lower white matter scores in women, but not in men[37].

Through the use of imaging technologies such as PET and fMRI, disruption of subcortical reward systems as the underlying reason for addiction has given way to new theories of prefrontal cortex involvement via its regulation of reward regions of the brain as well as its involvement in executive functions such as self-control and awareness. Hence, damage to the prefrontal cortex leads to compulsive drug-taking, in part, via the individual's loss of free will[38].

---

35   Adinoff₃‘ B, Braud J, Devous MD, Harris TS (2012) Caudolateral Orbitofrontal Regional Cerebral Blood Flow is Decreased in Abstinent Cocaine-addicted Subjects in Two Separate Cohorts. Addiction Biology 17: 1001–1012.

36   Cheng GL, Liu YP, Chan CC, So KF, Zeng H, et al. (2015) Neurobiological underpinnings of sensation seeking trait in heroin abusers. Eur Neuropsychopharmacol 25: 1968-1980.

37   Monnig MA, Yeo RA, Tonigan JS, McCrady BS, Homa RJ, et al. (2015) Associations of White Matter Microstructure with Clinical and Demographic Characteristics in Heavy Drinkers. PLoS One 10: e0142042.

38   Goldstein RZ, Volkow ND (2011) Dysfunction of the prefrontal cortex in addiction: neuroimaging findings and clinical implications. Nature Reviews. Neuroscience 12: 652–669.

Conclusion

In cultures throughout the world, meditative practices have been used for centuries by devotees seeking ways to integrate mind and body and gain awareness and understanding of their inner and outer worlds.

Long shrouded in mystery and reserved for a small minority willing to undergo rigorous self-discipline over many years, abbreviated versions of these time-honoured traditions have been adapted for use in modern life, allowing practitioners to live and function in the modern world while receiving many of their life- and health-changing benefits. As science catches up with tradition, sensitive imaging techniques enable the visualisation of physiological changes as they occur in the brains and bodies of mindfulness practitioners, providing scientific proof where previously only empirical evidence existed.

Armed with a growing body of evidence, pilot programs designed around mindfulness techniques, some of which have been customised to the particular needs of certain groups, such as veterans with PTSD and addiction, have met with resounding success. The trend has even been labelled an "emerging phenomenon" by one researcher[39].

Some of the greatest benefits of mindfulness training have been seen in these populations, where the greatest need exists, and for which conventional drugs and psychotherapies have provided modest effects. Combining encouraging outcomes with the significant cost-savings and high safety profile of this low-tech therapy, it seems reasonable that mindfulness practices should continue to be integrated into mainstream treatment protocols in order to stem the growing tide of PTSD and addictions among veterans so that they may find hope, healing and joy in their lives.

If you find yourself trying to create perfectly stable surroundings or seeking to cultivate the external environment that you are lacking inside. If you are constantly consuming everything closest to you—food, love, validation—in an attempt to fill the void that you experience on a daily basis. That feeling of not

---

39   Cullen M (2011) Mindfulness-Based interventions: an emerging phenomenon. Mindfulness 2: 186-193.

being enough, of seeking desperately for the last piece of the puzzle, the piece that will round you out and make you whole and ease your pain.

Then consider that you no longer need to cover for your own imperfections, you can have the strength and courage to believe that you ARE repairable.

Don't stress yourself into thinking that if you become good enough, you can be transformed into a person deserving of a beautiful life. You already are deserving of a wonderful life, free of pain. YOU are the one your life is waiting for.

Vietnam Marine veteran Dan Burks says, "I could not believe what happened when I began meditating. It was the difference between heaven and hell. It was absolutely transformational."

YOU have the power to transform yourself.

Dr. Keerthy Sunder
February, 2022
https://doctorsunder.com/

Songs That Lead Me Through The Darkness

Why: Rascal Flatts

Jealous of the Angels: Donna Taggart

PIERUCCI
PUBLISHING
Elevating World Consciousness
Through Books.

What would a world look like where people choose to let their negative experiences make them STRONGER?

Pierucci Publishing is proud to facilitate books like "Outdance The Devil: A Soldier's Account of the Scariest Enemy He Ever Fought" because we believe that in order to enjoy a better world, we must create it.

Are you committed to elevating the world with your story? Contact us by visiting www.PierucciPublishing.com or calling us today at 855.720.1111.

Your story may be somebody else's survival guide.

With love,

Stephanie Pierucci

CEO, Pierucci Publishing
www.PierucciPublishing.com

Made in the USA
Monee, IL
17 April 2022

94921208R00128